BARKING
BUDDHA

BARKING BUDDHA

SIMPLE SOUL STRETCHES FOR YOGI AND DOGI

To Claire,
Wags + Woofs!
Brenda

BRENDA BRYAN
PHOTOGRAPHY BY BEV SPARKS

Henry

Gus

SKIPSTONE

Published by Skipstone, an imprint of The Mountaineers Books
Manufactured in Canada

First printing 2009
12 11 10 09   5 4 3 2 1

Copy Editor: Julie Van Pelt
Design: Mayumi Thompson

ISBN 978-1-59485-141-4

Library of Congress Cataloging-in-Publication Data
Bryan, Brenda.
  Barking Buddha : simple soul stretches for yogi and dogi / Brenda
Bryan ; photography by Bev Sparks.
    p. cm.
  ISBN 978-1-59485-141-4
  1. Dogs—Psychology. 2. Yoga. 3. Human-animal relationships. I. Title.
  SF433.B79 2009
  613.7'046—dc22

Skipstone books may be purchased for corporate, educational, or other promotional sales. For special discounts and information, contact our Sales Department at 800-553-4453 or mbooks@mountaineersbooks.org.

Skipstone
1001 SW Klickitat Way
Suite 201
Seattle, Washington 98134
206.223.6303
www.skipstonepress.org
www.mountaineersbooks.org

LIVE LIFE. MAKE RIPPLES.

I dedicate this book to my dogis, Honey and Gus.
They are my family, my best friends, my teachers, my heart.

CONTENTS

INTRODUCTION

Dog! When we first met on the highway of life, we came from the two poles of creation ...
What can be the meaning of the obscure love for me that has sprung up in your heart?
— ANATOLE FRANCE

TWO YEARS AGO, I was asked to provide dog massage at a Seattle Humane Society charity event at the Hotel Monaco downtown. The event was a doggie fashion show and I was there to give massage to the "models," all of which were dogs available for adoption. While there, I began talking with a representative from the Humane Society who was curious about the massages I was giving. I explained that I was a yoga instructor as well as a licensed massage therapist and devoted dog lover. The conversation ended with us discussing whether I could teach a dog yoga class at the Humane Society. One thing led to another, and I created Barking Buddha Doga, a yoga class that incorporates your dog into your practice.

While developing poses and meditations for Barking Buddha Doga, I realized that bringing your dog onto the yoga mat went beyond being quirky or cute. It actually makes a lot of sense. Traditional yoga practices are about creating a union with the divine in all. Dogs are pack animals, and pack mentality is also about union; in that sense, dogs are natural "dogis." Discovering union in a playful and fun way is what makes Barking Buddha Doga classes a unique

A Barking Buddha Doga class

Helping or hindering? Dogi and yogi attempt to Roll Over and Relax.

experience, giving both yogi and dogi an opportunity to connect in a new way.

Dogs can be enriching yoga partners because of that pack mentality, their emotional healing abilities, and their desire to be with their favorite humans. With their innate instincts, joy in simple pleasures, and soulful eyes, dogs also are seemingly enlightened beings—Barking Buddhas, if you will. From the sweet shelter dog, to the pampered toy breed in a sweater, to the misbehaving show dog, to the perfectly mannered mutt—our dogs teach us about life and love, each in his or her own way.

Dogs can help us open our hearts to the possibilities in relationships. We humans sometimes have difficulty learning or accepting from each other. But something about the "heart connection" we have with our dogs encourages us to uncover qualities in ourselves that we may otherwise have difficulty connecting to: unconditional love, letting go, being present, giving ourselves permission to play. Similarly, yoga practice can teach us about connecting to ourselves, learning awareness of our bodies and beings, so that we can better connect to others.

What if we were to bring our dogs onto our yoga mats, letting our dogs' natural abilities encourage openness and connection in us? Every dog is can do this, and every human can receive this from her dog.

The openness and connection is a deeply felt awareness that can be brought to the forefront of our lives through our yoga practice. And as we pursue this yogic path to health, fitness, connection, and entightenment, we can have a lot more fun by bringing our dogs with us.

Barking Buddha challenges you to call your dog to the yoga mat and let him lend a hand, or paw, as you embark (pun intended) on your spiritual journey.

The author and Gus teaching doga

SIT, STAY, RELAX: GETTING STARTED

If you eliminate smoking and gambling, you will be amazed to find that almost all an Englishman's pleasures can be, and mostly are, shared by his dog."
— GEORGE BERNARD SHAW

HOW DO YOU DO YOGA with your dog? The answer: You do doga. Doga is similar to yoga but turns it into a partner activity, but our partners aren't human—they're canine. When we bring them on the yoga mat with us, they become dogis. We approach this type of yoga practice a little differently, as you'll discover once you begin doing the poses in this book. The goals are similar to those of traditional yoga: union and self-awareness. The difference lies in the way we achieve that: using our canine companions as a catalyst for connection.

One common concern I hear is, "My dog isn't mellow enough for yoga." I hear this so often I have to consciously hold in a big frustrated sigh. If you are thinking the same thing (you know who you are), remember, it's *doga*. It's an activity with dogs, not a quiet spiritual meditation in an ashram on a sacred mountain. Though doga is a practice that can enhance any individual spiritual belief, it's one done with dogs, and dogs have their own ideas of a spiritual practice. Although most dogs react positively to doga at some point, some take longer than others to respond to the mellow vibe of the activity. If your dog takes a few sessions to settle in, don't worry. Just follow these tips to help your dogi enjoy being on the doga mat with you.

The primary purpose of Barking Buddha Doga is not to have a Zenned-out dog. Although that can be a by-product of the practice, for most people, doga is about spending time connecting and focusing on our relationship with our dogs, encouraging self-discovery, and having some fun. Hopefully, doga will benefit you and your dogi on the mat and off. Don't worry if you don't have a perfectly behaved dog. Your dog is perfect for *you* and your doga practice will evolve as he does.

To do doga, keep an open mind. This is most likely the first lesson your mutt monk will teach you. The second lesson is to let go of expectations. No matter how enlightened the souls of our dogs may be, our friends are still walking around in their four-legged, furry dog bodies. The third lesson is that practice makes perfect . . . maybe. Sometimes it takes a few sessions for certain high-energy dogs to get used to the mat. Dogs, like people and snowflakes, are all different; some will take to the mat right away, while others need encouragement.

BARKING BUDDHA GLOSSARY

DOG, n: A subsidiary Deity designed to catch the overflow and surplus of the world's worship . . . [H]is master works for the means wherewith to purchase the idle wag of the Solomonic tail, seasoned with a look of tolerant recognition.
—AMBROSE BIERCE

Heart Center: The metaphorical place where we feel. You know all the sayings: "broken heart," "my heart stopped," "bighearted," "bleeding heart," "kindhearted." All have to do with strong feelings from that virtually indescribable place within.

Intention: Ninety percent of accomplishments derive from where we focus our attention, where we focus our *intention*. The idea is to focus on a goal until it comes into being. Don't make this process laborious, just make it be. Think positively about what you want.

Mantra: From Sanskrit, an ancient East Indian language, *mantra* literally means "mind protector." A mantra is a word or phrase that we repeat over and over to focus the mind and prevent our thoughts from wandering from our intention.

Sit Bones: There are some phrases that you always hear in a yoga class but never hear outside of a yoga studio . . . this is one of them. The term *sit bones* is an easy way for a yoga teacher to describe the ischial tuberosities: the bony part of your butt that you sit on.

Here are some pointers:

1. **No treats during doga class.** Only use treats before and after the practice, followed by a short play session. If you bring treats into the session, your dog will become treat-obsessed. Use praise instead, and she'll get used to the mat and the practice and will soon associate the doga mat with time she gets to spend with you, her most favorite being! Of course, there are exceptions to every rule. Here is one: If your dog is very young or very high energy, you're probably still training her, so bring the training onto the mat by using treats. This will be effective during your at-home yoga practice, but if you decide to attend a group class, don't bring out treats during class time—unless you want all the other dogis to gather on your mat.

2. **Honor playtime.** Every day, bring your doga mat out for 5 minutes and allow playtime with toys and treats on the mat so your dog will associate doga with fun times with you. This should make a difference should you decide to attend a class

at a later date. After your dog is used to the mat, skip the treats and use praise and words of endearment as you begin your doga practice. This is especially great training for a puppy, because it teaches him to be comfortable with touch and stretching and to hang out with you quietly and confidently.

3. **Sometimes dogs bark and whine.** This happens because, well, they're dogs and this is how dogs communicate. Just like people, some dogs are more vocal than others. This behavior is more tolerated from a dog during doga practice than from a human during yoga class. Your dog will probably not continue this behavior after he learns what doga time means for him. He could just be expressing confusion about a new activity. Don't get discouraged. We all can feel confused when learning something new.

Head to Knee/Muzzle to Paw

MUTTLY MUDRAS

Dogs are miracles with paws.
—ATTRIBUTED TO SUSAN ARIEL RAINBOW KENNEDY

Mudras are used in yoga and meditation to re-direct the prana, or life force, in the body. The most common mudras are hand mudras, such as touching the index finger and thumb together—which people do to imitate a yogi.

In Barking Buddha Doga, we include our dogs in our mudras, directing prana to them and receiving it back. In this book, I've included four muttly mudras:

Puppy Paw Mudra: Use this mudra with the intention of grounding you and your dog in your practice, joining your intentions. Place your hands on top of your dog's front paws. This is a nice mudra to do in Puppy Child's Pose.

Heart-to-Hound Mudra: Place one hand on your heart and one on your dogi's chest or heart area. This is a sweet mudra that focuses your energy on the love you have for your dog and the love your dog has for you.

Inner Dog Mudra: Rest your forehead on your dog's forehead. In this mudra the intention is to open up to your dog's consciousness and connect the energy of your minds.

Barking Buddha Mudra: Place one hand on your dogi's head or upper back and your other hand on his low back. Use this mudra to give healing energy to your dogi and to receive healing energy from your dogi.

Puppy Paw Mudra

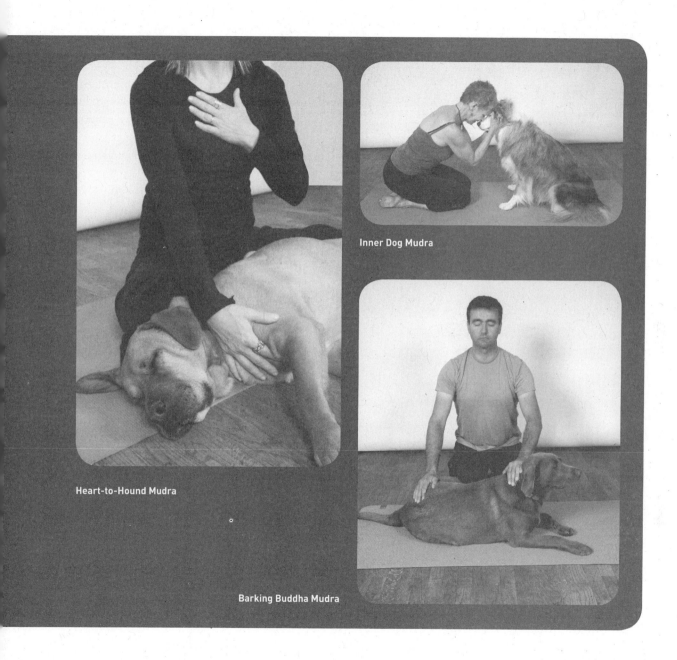

Heart-to-Hound Mudra

Inner Dog Mudra

Barking Buddha Mudra

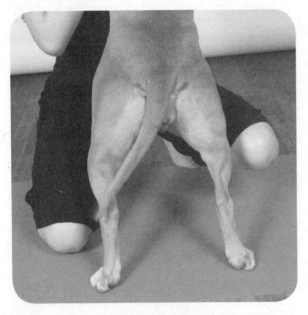

Like humans, every dog has a different level of fitness.

4. **Be aware of your physical condition and your dog's.** This book is for beginners, but everyone and every dog has a different level of fitness, so don't push it. If you have a large, older dog or a dog with a long spine (like a dachshund), be particularly careful and mindful in poses that call for lifting your dog. If your instincts say "no," listen to that and do the modification suggested.

5. **Enhance your practice.** The poses in this book are designed for beginners and are grouped for use as individual thematic sessions. It also can be helpful, however, to use the poses from "Gratitude" as a quick warm-up. If you do so, omit the meditation at the end and simply move into the poses of your choice from one of the other chapters.

6. **Have fun.** Enjoy your dog—every woof-woof, bark, pant, and sniff!

GRATITUDE

When the Man waked up he said,
"What is Wild Dog doing here?"
And the Woman said,
"His name is not Wild Dog any more,
but the First Friend,
because he will be our friend
for always and always and always."
—RUDYARD KIPLING

I'M GRATEFUL FOR THE RELATIONSHIP I have with my dogs, Honey and Gus, and I'm thankful for the amazing dogs I meet in my Barking Buddha Doga classes. The fact is, dogs rock my world and make everything better! And as I experience doga with my dogs and deepen my relationship with them through our time together, I've started to believe that my dogs, and all dogs, are naturally enlightened beings.

The everyday stuff that comes easily to them can feel a little challenging to me because I let my human-ness get in the way. Even if it's just an hour's romp at the dog park or a ride in the car, dogs adapt and quickly figure out their role. They have a natural, simple wisdom to just be: their "dogdom." I'm thankful for this dogdom, because it puts me in touch with my inner dog and keeps me from taking myself too seriously. Dogs remind me to embrace life's simple pleasures—like a bowl of good food, a treat, a sunny day, soft grass, kind words, and most importantly . . . playtime.

I'm grateful for how dogs influence our lives as natural healers, a quality that became clear once I started bringing Honey and Gus into my yoga practice. Their presence opened my heart in a deep and pro-found way. I've also noticed that others experience this kind of healing while being around dogs—not just dog owners, but folks who simply interact with dogs.

Every dog takes on a role in her lifetime as a healer and teacher to help us open our hearts. Even dogs that suffer from a lifetime of abuse have sacrificed their well-being in their short, painful lives so that we can open our hearts to deep feelings of compassion or a call to positive action. We discover this, perhaps, by adopting a rescue dog and teaching her to love and trust again, while awakening these feelings in ourselves. Or maybe a shelter employee or volunteer begins to un-derstand deeper levels of patience, perseverance, and unconditional love through the homeless or abused dogs he or she encounters.

Double Dog Down Dog

The moment we begin to open our hearts to what our canine companions can offer us, healing and awareness can start. It doesn't need to be complicated. Often it's as simple as the way your dog's goofy behavior can turn your frown into a smile. Dogs often force us outside of our ego and personal drama by reminding us to honor the unspoken contract we've made to love, honor, and care for them. If this sounds as important as another type of partnership agreement many of us make, it is!

So to begin our doga practice, I offer my sincere gratitude to dogs everywhere for what they bring to us as natural healers, teachers, and enlightened beings. Thank you.

BARKING BUDDHA POSES FOR GRATITUDE

The poses for Gratitude are simple positions designed to introduce you and your dog to a newfound union within this yoga practice—in the same way that feelings of gratitude are simple and pure and often show us the best part of ourselves. I believe our dogs live in this place of gratitude and union all the time and they remind us to find this inner truth in ourselves by connecting us to these feelings. Consider doing these poses on their own or, as you get more comfortable, as a warm-up to other sets of poses.

Seat with a Treat

Sit on your knees, tops of your feet on the floor; your sit bones should rest comfortably on your heels. (You can also sit in a comfortable cross-legged position with your dog on your lap—Dogi-Yogi Easy Pose—if you have knee problems.) Your doga partner sits in front of you on the yoga mat.

Place your left hand on your dogi's right shoulder and your right hand behind your sit bones on the floor.

DOGI: GUS

Age: 6

Breed: Gus is lovingly described by his yogi as "fourteen-pound mystery meat." He likely has some silky terrier in him, and perhaps some papillon.

Yogi: Brenda

Gus was adopted before he was born, after his mother arrived pregnant at Fur Baby Rescue in Blaine, Washington. A few weeks after his birth at this shelter specializing in small-dog rescue, he met his yogi. Gus loves to mingle at parties—and enjoys watching the sunset on the beach.

Seat with a Treat

Lift the front of your spine as you gently twist from your low belly. Relax your shoulders.

While you breathe in the pose, explore the shape of your dog's right shoulder, noticing where the muscle connects to the bone, feeling the shape and size of the muscle. Notice your dogi's breathing, her inhales and exhales. Gently massage your dog's shoulder as you breathe in your twist. You can do this by making gentle circles on the shoulder with your fingertips or entire hand, depending on the size of your dog.

On the inhale, unwind the twist, lift your sit bones, coming to stand on your knees, and then exhale the sit bones back down to your heels as you sweep your right hand to your dog's left shoulder and your left hand behind you.

Do this pose two or three times on each side before moving to Camel Rides Dog.

Camel Rides Dog

Stand on your knees, knees hip distance apart. If you have a small dog, you can place your dog between your knees. If you have a large dog, he can be in front of your knees, touching the front of your thighs. Tuck your tailbone and lift the front of your spine from below your belly button.

Your dogi will help with awareness of your lengthening tailbone as you squeeze your knees slightly and gently inward. *Gentle* is the key word: Please don't squish your doga partner by squeezing your knees too hard.

Place your hands on your hips or low back and continue, lengthening the front of your spine, lifting your belly and heart. Squeeze your shoulder blades together

Camel Rides Dog, large dog variation

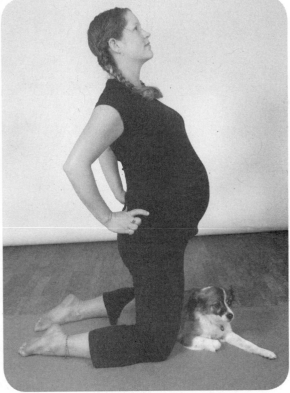

Camel Rides Dog, small dog variation

as you lift your heart up to the ceiling so you have a nice stretch in your chest and shoulders. Really taco in those shoulder blades, like those old-school hard-shell tacos that mom used to make on Mexican food night.

Take a few mindful breaths and then move up and back into Double Dog Down Dog.

Double Dog Down Dog

Start on your hands and knees, hands shoulder distance apart, your dogi in between your hands or in front of you. This pose is easier if your dogi lies down. Tilt your pelvis up so that your sit bones are lifted high to the sky. Keep that lift in your sit bones as you curl your toes under and move your hips up and back, extending your heels toward the ground. Push forward with the roots of your fingers to extend your arms and bring the weight of your body back into your legs.

Remember how your dogi yawns into her morning stretch with her front legs extended out and her butt in the air. This is how the pose should look and feel.

Double Dog Down Dog, large dog variation

It's okay if your heels don't touch the ground; that just means the backs of your legs are tight from sports, life, or wearing high heels (and I'm personally not willing to give up that extra height from a gorgeous pair of shoes!).

Corkscrew your elbows in, opening up your elbow creases, and feel how that broadens your upper back. Now relax your neck, bringing the crown of your head to rest on or in the direction of your dog, symbolically joining your intentions—let your dog help you deepen your stretch by doing this.

After taking some nice deep breaths in Double Dog Down Dog, come back down to your knees to rest in Puppy Child's Pose.

Puppy Child's Pose

This is a resting pose and one of the sweetest of the practice because it brings your heart close to your dog. It's ideal if the dogi is lying down. (If he's not, try any restful position that allows you gentle contact.)

From your hands and knees, simply move your sit bones back to your heels. As you bend your knees, let your belly come in between your thighs. Your dogi can be between your knees; if your dog is large, it's fine if your knees are a little wider apart.

Rest your cheek on your doga partner and listen to her breath. Try to feel from your heart by allowing your heart to open with the love you feel for your dog. Remember that the purpose of yoga, and doga,

Puppy Child's Pose

is union, and this pose is a perfect example of what it feels like to be connected to gratitude and love.

You can meditate in this position, or come to a comfortable seat to move into a meditation on gratitude.

MEDITATION FOR GRATITUDE

Sit comfortably with your dogi—cross-legged on a little height, or with your back against the wall, or on a chair with your hands on your knees—whatever is most comfortable for you. Become aware of your breath by focusing on your inhales and exhales as they enter and exit your body through your nostrils. Your mouth should be gently closed and your face and shoulders relaxed. Become aware of your dogi's inhales and exhales.

As you sit breathing quietly with your dogi, begin mentally offering gratitude for all the things your dog gives to you—emotionally, spiritually, physically—all that she brings into your world everyday. Companionship. Love. Play. Anything that comes to mind that you are grateful for. Let this feeling of gratitude begin to expand out from your heart in all directions, surrounding you and your dog with an intention of gratitude.

Continue breathing into your heart center and begin to expand the feelings of gratitude into all areas of your life—family, friends, work, your garden, a bike ride, things that bring you happiness, or even not-so-happy situations that allow for more growth and self-awareness. Whatever comes to mind, surround it with gratitude, moving that intention out in all directions, sharing it with the universe.

After this feels complete, open your eyes and say "thank-you" to your dogi. Now give her a treat, and notice the expression of gratitude on her wise and sweet face.

UNCONDITIONAL LOVE

I think dogs are the most amazing creatures; they give unconditional love. For me they are the role model for being alive.

—GILDA RADNER

I REALLY LOVE MY DOGS in a huge heart-busting, wide-open way. I'm strict with them when I need to be (absolutely no begging allowed while we're eating), and lenient at other times (please come up on the couch and snuggle close). I love Honey and Gus as my dog children, even on those rare occasions when they misbehave.

I still loved Gus just as much when I had to retrain him to "go" outside after we moved from the only house he'd ever known. Stepping in poop in my own home—barefoot—although frustrating and, yes, gross, didn't change my feelings for little Gus. I still loved him unwaveringly throughout the retraining process.

But I have to ask: Do Honey and Gus love me unconditionally? Or am I choosing to believe that my love is reciprocated because it makes me feel good? They seem happy to see me when I arrive home and they frequently seek out my company, if not my lap, when I'm home. If I'm angry or upset, they look up at me with what I perceive as a big-eyed look of concern. Are these signs of unconditional love? Because they don't speak English and I only speak a little dog, I have to take a lot for granted.

I know what you're thinking. I'm a sucker. I'm their meal ticket. The dogs aren't happy to see me come home because I'm a fabulous and entertaining person and they're overwhelmed with feelings of undying devotion . . . they're just hoping I'll fill their empty food dishes. They seek me out because I have opposable thumbs that enable me to prepare food for them. The tail wagging and snuggles on the couch are actually requests for rawhide bones or a treat, or maybe they just need to be let outside. My fear has been if Honey and Gus were faced with the choice between a big steak or a big hug from mom, I could be left with empty arms and no big-eyed looks of concern. Even the idea of this truth hurts, and this unconditional love thing is something I've thought about a lot. With all the information we've been given recently about pack life and what dogs really need to be fulfilled as dogs—from documentaries on cable TV to the many dog-training books available—where is the love?

Some theories don't give much weight to the relationship between a dog and his person, saying that the dog owner's primary mission should be to establish dominance as the pack leader. For me, though, the relationship is more symbiotic. I do think it's important that we be the pack leaders, because it gives our furry loved ones the freedom to live their dogdom to the fullest without the pressure of being the boss. That's our job and dogs love that we do it as long as they *understand* what's expected of them. My own theory is that our dogs can flow as fulfilled pack members while retaining the sweetness of a loving relationship with their humans.

I like to believe that, somewhere beneath that pack-dog mentality, there's a soul I connect with on a level that goes deeper than the food dish. I believe that my dogs and I came together in this lifetime for a purpose—to be companions and to play, learn, and love together. Dogs are here to assist us in opening our hearts so that we can experience things like unconditional love. I like my theory because it means that I am loved unconditionally by my dogs and they know how much I love them too. Our souls are meant to experience love in this life we share together.

BARKING BUDDHA POSES FOR UNCONDITIONAL LOVE

These poses help open the chest and shoulders. As we release tension in the chest and shoulders, we're able to breathe a little freer and feel a little deeper. As you and your dog flow through this sequence, let your open chest and shoulders symbolize an opening of the heart center, where we connect with feelings like unconditional love.

Seat with a Treat

Sit on your knees with a straight spine and your butt on your heels, tops of your feet on the floor. If you have troublesome knees, sit in Dogi-Yogi Easy Pose—a crossed-legged position on the floor with your dog by you or on your lap.

DOGI: HONEY

Age: 11
Breed: Shar Pei–boxer mix
Yogi: Brenda
When she was four years old, Honey was handpicked for her yogi. She enjoys stuffed animals and a good chew bone. She also loves to sit on her yogi's lap, and even though she is almost fifty pounds, her yogi doesn't mind. She's a little wrinkly and a lot sweet.

Seat with a Treat

Lift your belly and chest as your shoulders release down your back, and place your right hand on your dogi's left shoulder. Feel her shoulder muscle, the shape, where it inserts in the bone, and the quality of the tissue. Using a gentle circular squeezing motion with your hand, begin to massage your dogi's shoulder.

Sweep your left hand behind your back, placing it on the floor so that you're in a twist. Keep your spine straight and try to twist from your low belly.

Repeat on the other side by placing your left hand on your dogi's right shoulder and your right hand on the floor behind you. Stay for a few breaths, releasing each side of your spine as you release your dogi's shoulder muscle.

Puppy Play

This pose is somewhere in between Puppy Child's Pose and Double Dog Down Dog. Start in Puppy Child's Pose with your dog in front of you. Bring your hands to the floor, arms extended on either side of your dog.

As you extend your arms and draw your shoulders back, lift your sit bones and engage your belly by drawing your navel slightly up and in. Basically, mimic that bow pose your dogi does when she wants you to play with her.

While in the pose, smile at your dogi, squinting your eyes, then rest your forehead on her. The intention here is to connect the minds and hearts of dogi and yogi.

If you would like to move into Double Dog Down Dog from here, curl your toes under, keep your arms extended, and lift your sit bones high as you straighten your legs, moving your heels to the floor. The intention is the same: a heart connection. Even if this is not something you can fully grasp on an intellectual level, just think "heart connection" and you'll begin to feel instead of think.

Breathe here with your dogi for as long as you like, then come back to a seated position to prepare for Flying Dog.

Puppy Play, large dog variation

Flying Dog

From a seated position, place your feet on the floor in front of you, hip distance apart. Place your hands on the floor behind you, fingers pointed in the direction of your feet. If you have a small dog, place her on your belly; a larger dog can be under your knees.

Squeeze your shoulder blades together and reach your heart forward, creating a nice shoulder and upper

Flying Dog, small dog variation

back stretch. If you want more of a stretch, tuck your tailbone and lift your pelvis off the floor, keeping your chin slightly tucked so you don't strain your neck.

Go slowly, especially if your dogi is on your belly. She may try to jump off the first time, but once she gets the hang of it, she'll fly into the pose with you.

Flying Dog is a nice heart-opening pose and it works the arms and the glutes.

MEDITATION FOR UNCONDITIONAL LOVE

I've read that dogs don't enjoy being hugged because it's a sign of dominance. But hold on: Here's another theory I have about dogs. Although I wouldn't hug a strange dog, I think dogs enjoy the closeness of a hug from their person. I often "group hug" my dogs to let them know that we're in this together (cue the Pointer Sisters and sing "We are fam-il-y!").

I also notice that dogs "hug" in their own way. My dog Honey likes to lean on me with all of her weight, even putting her head on my chest or shoulder; I call this her dog hug. Gus is smaller, and he hugs in a similar manner, but sometimes he'll be on my lap during hug time.

Hug meditation, small dog variation

Hug meditation, large dog variation

So while we meditate on unconditional love with our dogis, let's get close to them—hug your dog if it's comfortable and if your breath can flow easily, or just sit close.

Intention is a big part of manifestation. Let the intention of love for your dogi help you in opening your heart to feelings of unconditional love. Then let that loving feeling become one of compassion and loving-kindness toward all beings. We don't have to like everyone, but we can love the part of them that is doing the best they can. We can extend love and compassion to others with the awareness that, like us, they have their own experiences and their own path to follow—different, but just as important as ours. In this way we are all connected and we can begin to feel unconditional love not only for ourselves and our loved ones but also for the soul of all humanity and all living things.

Let your dogi help you with this as you breathe with the mantra: May I be as loving to myself as I am to my dog. Then move into: May I be as loving to all as I am to my dog.

After your meditation, give your dogi a sincere "I love you" and hug. Kiss her on the top of her head, and don't forget her post-doga treats!

Puppy Play, small dog variation

PERSPECTIVE

All knowledge, the totality of all questions and all answers, is contained in the dog.
— Franz Kafka

ONE OF THE VERY FIRST THINGS I learned from teaching doga is to let go of expectations—to try to see things from other points of view, to wag my tail in a new direction, so to speak.

During one Sunday class at the Humane Society, Buddy, a large, handsome pit bull, was barking continuously. At first I was a little irritated, talking loudly to be heard over Buddy's vocals. This went on for some time—Buddy barking, me barking louder. I was having a conversation in my head with Buddy that was completely different than what I was teaching. "Shut up, relax, and enjoy the class," I was telling him. Then I had a smack-on-the-head moment: Maybe Buddy *was* enjoying the class. Maybe a dog's idea of a fulfilling doga class was different from my idea of a perfect class. Buddy was quite possibly having a wonderful time. He was expressing his dogdom by barking and was saying some important stuff, I'm sure. Yes, we should teach our dogs not to bark obsessively, but this dog was here to teach *me*. This dog was here to change my perspective on what makes a good doga class, because as Buddy was trying to tell me, it's not just about me and the human students, it's also about the dogs.

In my ideal doga class, dogs and humans work side by side peacefully and quietly on the path to enlightenment. But for Buddy and other dogs, a good class means hanging out with mom or dad, seeing other dogs, getting petted, having treats at the beginning and end of class, barking a little, and playing. I needed to change my perspective. I needed to walk the walk. In the little speech I give at the beginning of each class, I claim that even if you are doing something different than everyone else in the room, you're still practicing doga and spending quality time connecting. I realized I needed to own that speech and apply it liberally to my role as instructor.

Fortunately, I learned this lesson early in my doga teaching career, because I've been faced with other Barking Buddhas in the class as well as in the next room at the various dog facilities where I teach. (You thought these classes took place in a quiet, incense-filled sanctuary of a yoga studio? Hah!) Not all of the classes are loud, but now whenever I'm practically yelling to teach over the noise of dogs being dogs, I'm also trying not to laugh as I assure the alarmed human students that the dogs are, well, just being dogs. As a teacher, I can use the situation as a way to talk about expectations and allowing for new perspectives: When you're able to see something differently, you give the universe permission to shift the energy around your circumstances. It's like taking a nice deep breath and releasing a full exhale. You can release an old pattern or way of thinking, and make room for a new perspective or renewed clarity.

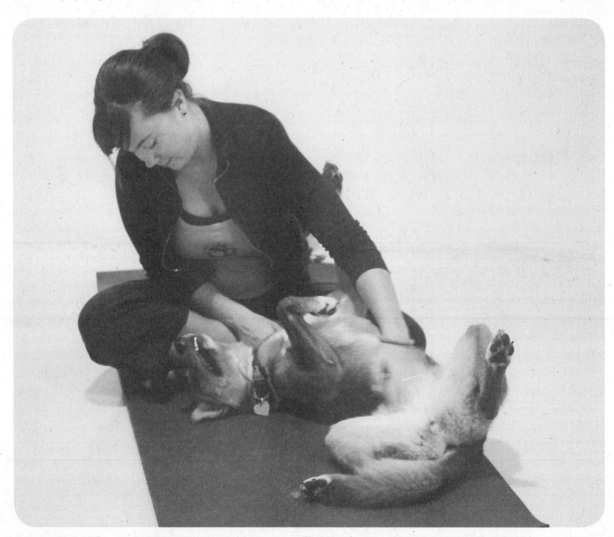

A relaxed moment on the doga mat

DOGI: JINXI

Age: Approximately 2
Breed: Chihuahua–Shiba Inu mix
Yogi: Darren
Sweet, energetic, and a natural at doga, Jinxi found her yogi via Ginger's Pet Rescue, which specializes in saving dogs on death row. Jinxi was saved from a kill shelter in California.

So when life gives us a barking dog, we have to remember it's not the barking we should give our attention to, it's how we respond to the dog barking that can lead us to change our perspective in any given situation.

BARKING BUDDHA POSES FOR PERSPECTIVE

Challenge yourself to view life from your dog's perspective as you move together from pose to pose. This will help you focus on your intention and prevent you from getting stuck in any one thought pattern.

Double Dog Down Dog

Start on your hands and knees, hands shoulder distance apart, your dogi between your hands or in front of you. This pose is easier to do if your dogi is lying down.

Tilt your pelvis up so that your sit bones are lifted high to the sky and your spine is curved with your belly reaching down. Keep that lift in your sit bones as you curl your toes under and move your hips up and back, extending your heels toward the ground. Push forward with the roots of your fingers to extend your arms and bring the weight of your body back into your legs.

Corkscrew your elbows in, opening up your elbow creases, and feel how that broadens your upper back. Think about how your dog yawns into his morning stretch with his front legs extended out and his butt in the air. This is how the pose should look and feel.

Double Dog Down Dog, small dog variation

Now relax your neck, bringing the crown of your head to rest on or in the direction of your dogi, symbolically joining your intentions. Let your dogi help you deepen your stretch.

After taking some nice deep breaths in Double Dog Down Dog, begin to walk your feet toward your hands into a forward bend, what we call Up-Tail in Barking Buddha Doga. Bend your knees on the way if it makes the transition easier.

Up-Tail to Half Up-Tail with Wheelbarrow

Up-Tail, like Double Dog Down Dog, is an inversion. Inversions are good for memory and concentration and seeing things in a new way by turning your world upside down.

Begin with your toes pointed forward, standing with feet hip distance apart, your dogi in front of you facing away from you. With hands on your hips, squeeze your shoulder blades together, lifting your heart and belly before folding over into a forward bend, or Up-Tail.

34

Half Up-Tail

As you fold from your hip crease's and hang your spine from your pelvis, place your hands on your dog and move the crown of your head toward your dogi. Ideally, the crown of your head will rest on your dog, especially if she is standing, but it will depend on her height and your flexibility.

Move your weight slightly forward. Breathe with your dogi in Up-Tail, letting the energy from the crown of your head open up symbolically to assist you in shifting perspective.

Now place your hands on either side of your dogi's shoulders and lift your chest up until your spine is parallel to the ground, into Half Up-Tail. Tuck your tailbone and lift your belly up and in, and begin to fold down again, back into Up-Tail, as you let your hands travel down your dog's sides to her hips. As you fold over into full Up-Tail, let your hands slide down your dog's back legs to her paws, your firm touch increasing the blood flow in her hips and back legs.

Wheelbarrow, small dog variation

Wheelbarrow, large dog variation

Being mindful of your dog's age, weight, and health, you can give her a nice hip stretch in Wheelbarrow by lifting her back legs from right beneath her hip creases. (Do not lift her up by grabbing the middle of her legs; it's uncomfortable and not a good, stable dogi stretch.) Keep your core firm by tucking your tailbone and lifting your belly up and in. If your dog is on the taller side you will usually end up moving back up to Half Up-Tail. Gus loves this stretch and will push into the front of my legs to enhance his stretch and lengthen his spine. It's so cute!

Now carefully release your dogi's back legs to the ground, moving into full Up-Tail. As you move into your forward bend and you feel yourself physically shifting down and forward, release all expectations. Allow the gentle, presence of your dog to assist you as you bring your intention to a shift in perspective. Let this pose not only shift your physical perspective but also your mental perspective, allowing the energy to move to an area where you feel stuck in your life. Let your awareness of your dog as a different species, with her own perspective coexisting with you harmoniously, help you make the shift physically and mentally between poses.

MEDITATION FOR PERSPECTIVE

Double Dog Down Dog and Up-Tail poses literally change your physical perspective. Now you want to shift perspective to an area in your life where you might feel stuck.

Sit comfortably with your dog and hold both of his ears in between your thumb and index finger. Starting at the base of his ears, make very gentle circles around the edges of his ears from front, to

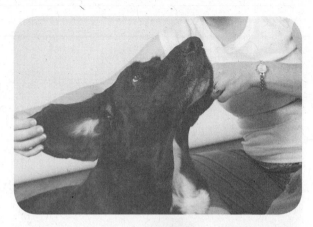

Ear massage meditation

tip, to back. Then massage the whole ear using your fingertips and thumb. This gentle work stimulates the acupressure points in your dogi's ears; you have them in your ears too.

Our inner voice is that part of us that is connected with the wisest and truest element of our decision-making abilities. This voice is different from the pesky, doubting ego voice because it's guided by the best part of ourselves. It's that knowing within that feels connected to all things and moves confidently through life in love and wisdom, not fear and drama.

As you begin to activate the acupressure points in your dog's ears, bring your attention to him and let the action activate your own ability to listen to your inner voice. In doing so, you will shift your perspective in a positive direction to face life's challenges with more clarity and confidence.

Sit quietly and relax in this awareness for a few moments with your dogi after the ear massage. Breathe and listen. Then thank your beautiful dogi for helping you shift your perspective by giving her a treat, and finish today's doga session with a fresh point of view.

DOGI: LUCY, A.K.A. "THE RUG"

Age: 11
Breed: Russian wolfhound
Yogi: Lynn

A retired double champion in confirmation and coursing, Lucy came to her yogi after her training days were over—and after nursing a litter of ten pups! She is a sight hound, drawn to the slightest movement of prey (a squirrel, cat, or raccoon), but now she only wants to keep Lynn in her sight. One of Lucy's daughters, Fionna, also was adopted by Lynn and will soon take up doga too.

FOCUS

Dogs have given us their absolute all. We are the center of their universe. We are the focus of their love and faith and trust. They serve us in return for scraps. It is without a doubt the best deal man has ever made.

—Roger Caras

WHEN BEV SPARKS VISITED one of my Barking Buddha classes to photograph the session, I was impressed by the complete concentration that Lulu, one of my dog students, showed. Sadly, Lulu wasn't focused on me, but rather on the possibility of getting a treat from Bev. Lulu remained standing the entire class, watching every move Bev made. Almost without exception, even the most rowdy dog will settle down by the end of class, lying down and responding to the mellow vibe of the class. But Lulu could not take her eyes off Bev. She was riveted for the entire hour.

After class, Lulu's owner told me that Lulu knew Bev would give out treats because of a previous experience of having her picture taken with Bev. Wow. This dogi had more focus during her practice than many experienced yogis I know. Treat . . . treat . . . treat . . . her very own doga mantra. I was impressed by this unerring and absolute attention. If I could bring this kind of focus into my own life, I could accomplish so much. Paint a masterpiece, stick to a diet, finish a home project! Maybe there's hope for me yet. Over the years, yoga has definitely helped me to focus. And now I can thank my dog student for reminding me to bring that intention back to my yoga and my doga practice. Good girl, Lulu—you deserve that treat!

BARKING BUDDHA POSES FOR FOCUS

This sequence includes balancing poses. Balancing poses require focus of the mind and the breath to keep stable and calm. Balancing poses are beneficial for feeling confident and sure in the way we move our bodies in sports, maneuver our dogs on challenging trails, or just stroll down the neighborhood sidewalk.

Dog in the Tree House

Begin standing with your dogi sitting or standing next to you. If your dogi is small, you can hold her in your arms for this pose.

Stand with your feet hip distance apart. Tuck your tailbone, but lift your belly muscles and your chest as you move your shoulders back and down. Standing on your right foot, bend your left knee and place your foot, toes pointing down, on your ankle, calf, or for the

Dog in the Tree House, small dog variation

Dog in the Tree House, large dog variation

most challenge, on your inner thigh. Keep opening your bent knee and stand taller.

Your small dog is held next to your heart and your large dog is standing or sitting under your bent knee, assisting you in your balance by focusing on her own stay as you gaze in her direction. If your dogi is next to you, bring your hands together at your heart. Focus your attention on the love you have for your dog and know that she loves you too.

Stay for three to five breaths. Repeat the pose on the other side, or for more of a flowing sequence, do the next two poses before moving to the other side.

Dog Is My Copilot

This is another balancing pose that also works the hamstrings. For this pose, place your dogi in front of you. Stand tall with your core engaged by tucking your tailbone and lifting your belly up and in—a strong core

Both yogi and dogi need focus to practice doga.

will help you feel more stable in your balancing poses.

Bring your weight to your right leg. As you slightly bend your right knee, begin to hinge forward at your hips, reaching your arms toward the floor and extending your left leg out behind you. Keep the toes of your back leg pointing down so that your hips are square to the floor. Don't scrunch your shoulders as you bring your hands to the floor.

If you feel stable, rest one hand on your dog, not on her spine but on her shoulder or hip. If, and only if, you are feeling very balanced, you can rest both hands lightly on your dog so that she can help you focus on your balance.

If you are comfortable here, you can work toward straightening your standing leg for more of a hamstring stretch. If you choose to keep one hand or both hands on the ground, focus your gaze on your dogi to assist you with your balance as you breathe in the pose.

Another way to do this pose is to come to your hands and knees, with one knee on the ground and your opposite leg extended behind you.

After you've held the pose for a few mindful, focused breaths, set your left leg and knee on the ground with your toes curled under, bending your right knee into a lunge. You're ready to flow right into the next pose. Don't forget to come back and do the poses on the other side.

Dog Is My Copilot

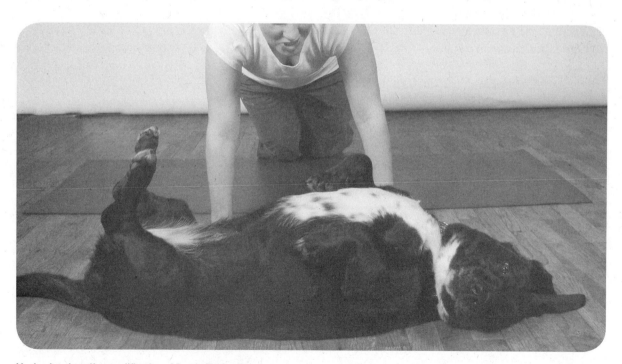

Moving into kneeling modification of Dog Is My Copilot

Super Dog Twist with Lunge

From your low lunge—left knee on the ground or lifted, depending on your flexibility, balance, and energy level—bring your dogi to the inside of your right knee. Tuck your tailbone and lift your belly up and in to engage your core. Draw your inner thigh muscles toward each other for more stability in your lunge.

Now lift your dogi from underneath her front armpits, right at the armpit crease, which should extend her front legs out in front of her. This gives her a nice stretch (and it looks really cute). If your dog is too large to lift, massage under her armpits and down her front legs as you breathe in your lunge.

If she is fine while lifted up and with her front legs extended, then move your torso slightly to the right so that her torso is also twisting slightly to the right—not a big movement at all. Now twist gently to the left.

Repeat all of the Barking Buddha Poses for Focus on your second side, and then sit comfortably with your dogi for our doga meditation.

MEDITATION ON FOCUS

In yoga, sometimes we use a mantra to bring focus back to our practice. You can use a mantra with your breath as you move through the doga poses, or to focus attention in meditation.

As you sit quietly with your dogi, your dog's name can become a meaningful mantra. Repeat your dog's name over and over again with your breath. For example: Inhale "Lola," exhale "Lola." You could also use the phrase "I love Lola" on the inhale and "Lola loves me" on the exhale.

After feeling a sense of calm and focus from breathing your dog-name mantra, thank your dogi for helping you with your focus by giving her a well-deserved treat.

DOGI: LOLA

Age: 1½
Breed: Labrador retriever
Yogi: Mauricio
Lola loves her rubber chicken and swimming in the lake and will do just about anything for cheese.

Super Dog Twist with Lunge

JOY

In order to really enjoy a dog, one doesn't merely try to train him to be semi-human. The point of it is to open oneself to the possibility of becoming partly a dog.
— EDWARD HOAGLAND

AH YES, the pure and simple way our dogs experience joy. Sometimes just from a word or two: leash, treat, daddy's home. For Honey and Gus, I'm embarrassed to admit, the word *poopy* elicits pure joy because it means they get to go outside. (Curiously enough, word *bath* gets Honey pretty excited, but I'm not sure how that happened. The actual bathing of Honey does not give her joy, nor does she seem to even like it much.) The point is that dogs don't need much to be happy in the moment. They are ready to unleash (pun intended) pure joy at any given moment. A dog knows how to carpe their diem, and we can take a cue from canines by learning to experience joy as they do: simply and sincerely and in the moment.

Begin your quest for joy by getting in touch with your inner dog. Learn to be sincere in your happiness for small things, as they are. Then the bigger things that bring you joy will have space to manifest. This doesn't need to be complicated. Move toward living in joy by practicing joy. Start simply, by taking your dog on a walk and noticing the pleasure he finds in this simple activity. Bask in his pleasure and experience

Up-Tail pose, a forward bend, is used to move into and out of a variety of doga poses, including Half Up-Tail, Wheelbarrow, and Pit-to-Paw Standing Twist.

it for yourself through him. Make it easy like he does: smile, laugh, wag your tail, and feel that joy move through you from head to toe and muzzle to paw!

BARKING BUDDHA POSES FOR JOY

As you move through these poses, think about the things that bring your dog joy and how that in turn brings you joy. Remember to relax your face and jaw and let yourself smile as you breathe into each posture.

Pit-to-Paw Standing Twist

Because they release and untangle the spine, twists can help us begin to think about untangling situations in our lives that prevent us from feeling joy. Twists can also help detoxify the body because the twisting

Pit-to-Paw Standing Twist, with hand motion from shoulder to paw

DOGI: SUCIA

Age: 4
Breed: Her mother was an Australian shepherd mix, and her father's breed is unknown. He was possibly part coyote.
Yogi: Raederle

Sucia (pronounced su-sha) is a very special dog—so smart it's sometimes scary. You can't fool her for a moment. She is also a world traveler, having accompanied her yogi on a six-month-long road trip through Mexico. She enjoys practicing her doga at home and is a wonderful friend.

motion massages our organs. If we're sluggish from too many toxins, it's harder to experience the lightness that comes from being joyful.

Come into Half Up-Tail, feet hip distance apart and your torso hinged forward to bring your spine parallel to the ground—basically a half forward bend. Keep your belly firm. Let your right hand rest on your dog's left shoulder as you place your left hand on your low back, slightly twisting up to the left to open up your chest to that side of the room.

Take some lovely, deep breaths here as you make massaging circles on your dogi's shoulder. Remember to relax your own shoulders so you increase the opening of your chest and upper back.

After some breaths, inhale, and on the exhale let

your hand travel down your dogi's front leg from pit to paw as you move into a full forward bend, or Up-Tail. Bend at your hip creases and soften your knees if you need to. Then repeat the detoxifying twist on the other side.

Xtra Angle Triangle

Begin with your legs wide, about 3 feet apart. Turn your right foot out a little to the right so that its heel is in line with the center of your left foot. Gently tuck your tailbone and lift your belly up and in to engage your core, and spread your arms like bird wings. Reach your front (right) fingertips beyond your right foot to stretch your side and waist long as you open your heart and hips.

As your heart reaches open toward the ceiling, let

Xtra Angle Triangle, small dog variation

your top (left) hand reach up and your bottom (right) hand rest on your dog. You can also reach down and lift your dogi's paw so that his pose mirrors yours.

Bring your gaze down toward your dogi. Expand out in all directions, but keep your gaze and energy directed to your doga partner.

Repeat this joy-inducing, heart- and hip-opening pose on the other side.

Xtra Angle Side Angle with Twisting Dog, with hand motions around belly

Xtra Angle Side Angle with Twisting Dog

From Xtra Angle Triangle simply bend your right (front) knee so that it is directly over your ankle, even moving your knee out a little in the direction of your baby toe on your front foot. Lower your left (back) knee to the floor. Keep your chest open, tailbone tucked, and belly engaged. Place your upper hand on your hip and your lower hand on your dogi.

As you breathe in this pose, bring your attention to your doga partner. You've untangled your spine and massaged your organs with a twist; now it's his turn. Starting right under your dogi's front leg creases, hands on either side of your dog, begin to gently and lightly wring his torso, moving your hands down your dog's body with each wring until you come to his hips and belly. Be mindful in your touch and intent, feeling joy in this shared moment with your dogi as you assist each other in the poses.

Now change sides by inviting your other leg forward and coming into a low lunge on the other side.

Double Dog Down Dog

To continue releasing your upper back, shoulders, and spine, move into Double Dog Down Dog. With your hands on the floor, shoulder distance apart, your dogi between your hands or in front of you, tilt your pelvis up so that your sit bones are lifted high to the sky.

Keep that lift in your sit bones as you curl your toes under and move your hips up and back, extending your heels toward the ground. Push forward with the roots of your fingers to extend your arms and bring the weight of your body back into your legs.

Corkscrew your elbows in, opening up your elbow creases, and feel how that broadens your upper back.

Relax your neck, bringing the crown of your head to rest on or in the direction of your dog.

While breathing in this pose, embrace your inner dog and wag your tail. Yes, wag your tail by moving your hips back and forth. Go ahead and do it—no one's watching.

Double Dog Down Dog

Puppy Child's Pose

From Double Dog Down Dog, bend your knees and move your sit bones back to your heels. As you bend your knees, let your belly come in between your thighs.

Your dogi can be between your knees; if your dog is large, it's fine if your knees are a little wider apart. Rest your cheek on your doga partner and listen to his breath before moving to a comfortable seat for joyful meditation.

Puppy Child's Pose

MEDITATION FOR JOY

Sit cross-legged, and place your hands on your dogi or let him sit in your lap. Begin to envision all the things you do with your dog that bring the two of you joy: playing in the dog park, running on the beach, snuggling on the couch. Let everything else fall away.

If unpleasant thoughts come in, acknowledge them by saying silently, "Thanks, but no thanks. I don't need you right now." Then continue with thoughts of joy. Begin silently repeating the phrase "We feel joy." Smile. Rejoice in this beautiful relationship you have with your dog.

Sit in this joy and appreciation for as long as you like. When you have finished, thank your dogi for helping you to understand and feel true joy. Give him a dog biscuit and delight in his pleasure upon receiving his end-of-doga treat.

INSPIRATION

I hope if dogs ever take over the world, and they choose a king, they don't just go by size, because I bet there are some Chihuahuas with some good ideas.

—Jack Handey, "Deep Thoughts"

WHAT INSPIRES YOU? You probably have a good idea of what inspires your dog: food, treats, walks, toys, praise. But what inspires *you?*

I'm often inspired by the interactions I witness between humans and their dogs—not just in my classes but also in observing people playing with their dogs in the park or walking them downtown, offering them reassurance at the vet or letting them unabashedly hang their heads out the window of a moving car with tongues flapping in the wind.

Watching humans connect with their canine companions motivates me to be a better person and to do something in the world to foster more of that connection. Most humans I meet want to do the best they can to give their dogs a good life. And if they aren't sure of the best way to do it, the relationship and love they have for their dogs motivates them to move in that direction by learning and trying new things—like attending a doga class or taking a dog training course.

I myself have learned better dog training techniques and continued studying dogs, through books and other classes, so that I can help humans have the best relationship possible with their dogs. It's circular; people and dogs inspire me to learn more about people and dogs so that I can help them learn more about people and dogs . . . Did you get all that?

One way that I study dogs is to relax and observe. My doga practice gives me this opportunity. Time spent at ease watching my dogs or other people with their dogs instantly creates a relaxed space. Dogs seem to find this relaxation pretty easily, coming to their side-facing tummy pose almost anytime, anywhere (also known as Napping Position).

In a relaxed frame of mind, inspiration and creativity can more easily find us. When we are creative we're fulfilling ourselves as humans, and that makes us better people. We can use the time walking or playing or sitting with our dogs with the intention of encouraging this kind of relaxation and inviting inspiration.

So the next time you feel blocked or uninspired, let your dog help you. Hang out with her and observe. Play, go on a walk, and let the time relaxing with your dog take the pressure off, opening up space in your overworked brain for some true inspiration.

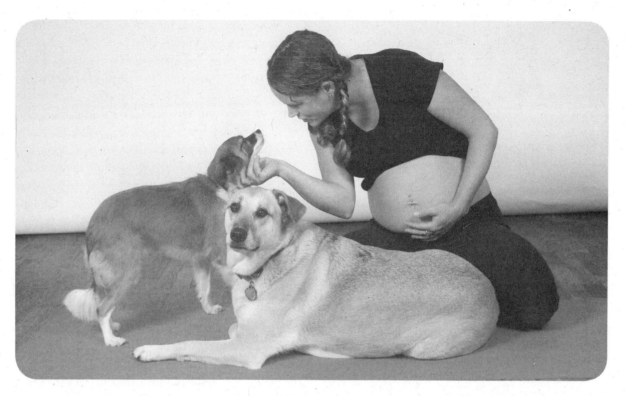

Dogs inspire us through their relaxed dispositions and interactions with us and each other.

BARKING BUDDHA POSES FOR INSPIRATION

As we open up our physical bodies with stretching, we begin to relax our minds by first relaxing our bodies. Stretching with our dogis inspires us to focus on the needs of another being and not just be caught up in our own needs and worries. This move away from what the Buddhists call "monkey mind" allows us to relax enough to expand into a more creative and inspirational existence.

You can do all the poses in this sequence one after another before moving to your other side for a more flowing style of practice, or you can do each pose on both sides before moving on to the next pose.

Doggy Door

Doggy Door is a nice back and leg stretch. It opens up the side of your body and gives your dogi a nice leg stretch as well.

Kneel on the floor with your dogi in front of you. As you stand on your knees, tuck your tailbone and lift your belly up and in so your core is nice and strong. Lift your chest and extend your right leg out to the side.

Doggy Door, large dog variation

Doggy Door, small dog variation

If you have a large dog, place your left hand on your dogi and extend your right arm up, leaning your torso to the left as your upper right arm reaches up and over, shadowing your right ear. Or gently reach under your dogi's front leg, right up in the crease, and slowly, gently lift—don't lift very much, just a little. Keep your belly slightly engaged and feel the nice stretch in your side waist and inner leg.

For a smaller dogi, lift up with both hands under his front legs, right under the pits, bringing your dogi to stand on his back legs as you mindfully extend his front legs à la Super Dog. Remember not to hold him up midleg; you always want to stretch from the leg pit (that is, of course, the official medical term).

Begin to lean slightly to the left, taking your little dog with you so he is leaning too. Keep your belly and heart lifted.

Hold the dogi stretch for one or two breaths and release him. You can keep your hand on your dogi and breathe in the pose for a couple more breaths if you would like to stay in the pose a bit longer.

Go directly into Doggy Door on your other side, or move into Double Dog Down Dog (see the Gratitude sequence) before moving to your other side.

Woofing Warrior 1

Let's energize our creative selves by doing Woofing Warrior 1 and 2. These poses open the chest and hips and strengthen the legs. They're standing poses, so they can also be very energizing.

Stand in a lunge with your left leg forward and your left knee directly above your ankle. Extend your right foot back and place it down at an angle, with the toes facing slightly forward. Square your hips so that your hip bones are shining straight ahead like

Woofing Warrior 1, small dog variation

Woofing Warrior 1, large dog variation

headlights. Tuck your tailbone as you lift your belly and heart.

Your small woofing warrior can be held in your arms or can sit on your front thigh, which will have the extra benefit of forcing you to bend your front knee a little more, working that leg muscle a little harder. Either way, you'll want to support your little dogi with

your left hand as you extend your right arm up, palm facing in toward your head.

Your large woofing warrior can be next to your front knee or under your front thigh, reminding you to keep your knee aligned over your ankle.

Breathe with your dogi. Notice how these strong Woofing Warrior poses inspire a sense of possibility and how your dogi is with you throughout—in the pose and out of the pose—helping you to relax your mind, body, and spirit and to move into inspiration and your desire to create.

Woofing Warrior 2

This pose is similar physically and in intention to Woofing Warrior 1. The difference is in the hips and chest. Instead of facing your hips and torso forward,

Woofing Warrior 2, large dog variation

Woofing Warrior 2, small dog variation

toward your front bent leg and the front of the room, open your hips and chest to the side of the room. Your tailbone is tucked and your heart and belly are lifted.

The same small/large dog modifications apply, except that your arms are outstretched like bird wings, palms facing down and shoulders moving down your back. If your dogi is in your arms or on your thigh, support him with your front hand and extend your back arm and hand.

MEDITATION FOR INSPIRATION

Sit comfortably with your dogi. Connect with your breath and then connect to his breath, noticing his inhales and exhales. As you focus on his breath, begin to release your worries and concerns from the day.

Continue to pay attention to your dogi's breathing and how his precious life force moves through him. You'll start to free your mind and relax. Bring a small Buddha smile to your lips as you think of what inspires your dog: Treats? Walks? Praise? Now let your mind and heart open to what inspires you. Visualize your inspiration in as much detail as possible.

Sit and be inspired with your dogi for as long as you like. After you've finished your meditation, give your dogi something that inspires him—a treat and a "good boy."

FAITH

I am I because my little dog knows me.

—GERTRUDE STEIN

HONEY AND GUS approach life in a pragmatic way. If they're sleepy, they sleep. If they're hungry, they eat. If someone comes to the door and threatens them everyday, they'll bark at that person everyday. (My poor mailman!) I tend to make things more complicated— weighing my choices, rationalizing, maybe overthinking a little (okay, sometimes a lot). Almost every decision, no matter how small, comes with a conversation in my head: French fries or salad? Buy the shoes, don't buy the shoes?

Honey and Gus seem to have pure faith that the choices they make are the right choices at the right time, even if that choice gets them a "bad dog," like chasing a squirrel or snatching that delicious sandwich off the coffee table. But what's really amazing is the faith they have in me. They have the confidence that I'll care for them and keep them safe.

Their belief in me as caretaker touches me deeply and gives me faith in myself to be the person they rely on. I once read of a man with a tattoo that said something like, "Lord, please help me to be the man my dog believes me to be." Like him, I want to be the fabulous, confident, wise person my dogs believe me to be in all situations. I want to take my dogs' simple faith in their dog choices and in me and apply that approach to my own life, tapping into my own inner wisdom. Then perhaps I can play the game of life with more confidence. I'll know that if I choose in the moment to eat that forbidden sandwich, I could earn a "bad dog." But maybe my choice will be different the next time. With each choice I'll reach a new level of self-discovery and I won't need a conversation in my head. I'll make the best decision for myself at the time as I embrace the mystery of life. I can move forward with faith that my choices will get better and better, with fewer "bad dogs" and more treats of self-assurance. Because I am, after all, the fabulous and wise person my dogs believe me to be.

BARKING BUDDHA POSES FOR FAITH

These three poses can bring awareness of the faith our little dogs have in us, because they'll be physically supported by us in the poses. Our larger dogs will be our faithful companions as they lie in napping pose under our knees.

Floating Dog

Start with Floating Dog, which works the core. Sit on the ground with your legs in front of you, knees bent and feet on the floor, hip distance apart. Your small dog is on your belly, or your large dog is under your knees.

Floating Dog, small dog variation

Floating Dog, large dog variation

Engage your belly and keep your chest lifted and shoulders moving down your back. Keep your low back lifted as you slightly lean back until you feel your core working. This pose is more difficult if you have the extra weight of a small dog on your belly, but if you want even more of a challenge, lift your feet off the floor.

When your dogi has the faith that she won't fall off your belly, you can bring your arms loosely out to the sides, palms facing up or reaching toward your large dogi as he rests under your knees.

Stay for as many breaths as you like. It's common to feel a little shaky in this pose. That's just your core muscles letting you know they're working. Now you're ready to move into Flying Dog.

Flying Dog

From a seated position, put your feet on the floor in front of you, hip distance apart. Place your hands on the floor behind you, fingers pointed in the direction of your feet. If your small dogi is still on your belly after Floating Dog, you can keep her there; a larger dog can go under your knees.

Squeeze your shoulder blades together and reach your heart forward, creating a nice shoulder and upper back stretch. Tuck your tailbone and slowly lift your pelvis off the floor, keeping your chin slightly tucked so you don't strain your neck.

Remember to move slowly, especially if your dogi is on your belly. She may try to jump off the first time, but once she gets the hang of it, she'll fly into the pose with you.

Flying Dog is a nice shoulder-opening pose and it works the arms and the glutes. Stay for a few breaths. Then, you can do another Floating Dog, or roll your spine down until you're lying on the floor for Dog on Bridge.

Flying Dog, small dog variation

Flying Dog, large dog variation

DOGI: LULU

Age: 5
Breed: Boston terrier
Yogi: Bonnie

Lulu only likes to swim in shallow water, where she fetches a tennis ball by holding it down on the lake bottom with her paw. Then she dunks her head, like she's bobbing for apples, and triumphantly comes up with the ball in her mouth.

Dog on Bridge

Lie on your back with your knees bent, so they're pointing to the ceiling with your feet flat on the floor, hip distance apart. Your small dogi can be on your chest or belly, or your large dogi can be under your bent knees. Tuck your tailbone and slowly lift your pelvis off the floor, keeping your chest open by reaching your sternum to your chin, but not your chin to your sternum.

If your little dogi is comfortable staying on your belly during this pose without you holding onto her, you can roll your shoulders under and press your hands and arms into the ground to give you more lift in your backbend.

Backbending poses can inspire confidence, as your dogi faithfully waits for you to come out of the pose, rolling your spine down one vertebra at a time. Take your small dogi off your belly and lift your feet off the floor, bringing your calves parallel to the ground. Let your legs fall to the right as you come into a brief twist to release your spine after your backbend. Then let your legs go to the left, twisting to the other side.

Dog on Bridge, small dog variation

Dog on Bridge, large dog variation

Puppy Child's Pose

Briefly rest in Puppy Child's Pose before sitting for the meditation. Come to your hands and knees, and then bend your knees and move your sit bones back to your heels. As you bend your knees, let your belly come in between your thighs.

Your dogi can be between your knees; if your dog is large, it's fine if your knees are a little wider apart. Rest your cheek on your doga partner and listen to his breath before moving to a comfortable seat for your meditation on faith.

MEDITATION ON FAITH

Your dogi has helped you to understand the faith she has in you and the faith you have in your own abilities. Faith in yourself will enrich your relationship to everything around you, dogs and people alike. Having faith means delving into the unknown, embracing and experiencing where life takes you.

Begin the adventure now. Close your eyes and find Inner Dog Mudra by resting your forehead against your dogi's forehead. Be completely and totally present in this mudra with your dogi. Have the faith that whatever comes up—emotions, visual images, or new ideas—results from the energetic connection you have with your dog. Stay here and experience what it's like to have complete faith in what your relationship with your dogi can reveal to you if you allow yourself to be completely present with her and to believe.

When this meditation feels complete, thank your dogi and present your faithful friend and family member with her well-deserved after-doga biscuit.

EASE

I used to look at [my dog] Smokey and think, "If you were a little smarter you could tell me what you were thinking," and he'd look at me like he was saying, "If you were a little smarter, I wouldn't have to."

— Fred Jungclaus

THERE'S A YOGA POSE called Easy Pose. The Sanskrit name is Suhkasana, with the root *suhka*, or "ease." Easy Pose is simply sitting in a comfortable cross-legged position. For dogs, a position of ease is usually one of lying down. Halfway through my doga classes, most dogs lie down anyway, so it's not a challenging pose to get them into.

"The Rug" demonstrates an easy approach to Double Dog Down Dog.

There's one dog student I have named Lucy. Lucy is a retired show dog, a large borzoi who is as gentle as she is enormous. I've never even heard her bark. She was christened with the nickname "The Rug" after we noticed that throughout the entire class, no matter what her person or anyone else was doing, Lucy never moved. Even though the other dogis and yogis in the class were physically interacting as a team, Lucy was doing her own doga, content to chill out in her doggy Suhkasana: lying down, long, white fur splayed out around her, eyes half open, completely satisfied in the moment. Her human, Lynn, an accomplished yogi, could be doing anything around Lucy and she would continue to lie there, like a rug, relaxed and unaffected. I love this about my doga classes. Sometimes the yogis and dogis who outwardly don't

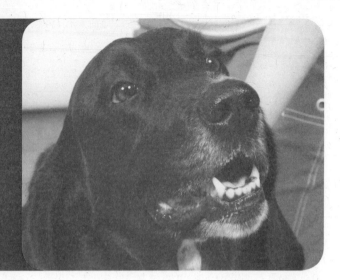

DOGI: MIA

Age: 6
Breed: Bassador (a basset hound–Labrador retriever mix)
Yogi: Rachel
Found via a basset rescue group, Mia is now a Delta Society Pet Partner, or therapy dog. She visits hospitalized children and works with at-risk youth. Her favorite treats are baby carrots.

seem to be doing all the perfect doga "moves" are actually expressing their doga in a profound way.

Lynn also brings Lucy to the yoga studio where I teach yoga. While Lynn is in class, Lucy assumes her same Suhkasana position on the big green couch in the lobby—eyes half open, fur splayed out. Sometimes she sighs. But mostly she stays in a Buddha-like state with her calm, watchful gaze, not a care in the world. Students walk by and talk to Lucy, pet her, sit next to her (although she doesn't leave a lot of room for company on the couch). And Lucy just hangs out, letting life happen with ease.

When we allow ease into our doga practice and into our lives, we can become like Lucy, calm and watchful as activity whirls around us. When we approach life with this kind of ease, it takes the pressure off. We can be like Lucy when she sighs as she lies on the couch while people walk by. She's acknowledging them, but not getting caught up and being influenced by their presence or actions.

If you can bring this kind of ease into your life, day-to-day struggles may feel less difficult. You can be more relaxed and in touch with what you want and can interact with others in a more positive way as situations arise—acting not reacting, whether life throws you a bone or sends you to the doghouse.

When we try to force things, we get stressed out, which tightens up everything around us, physically and energetically. When we practice ease and take a deep breath, our shoulders come down away from our ears and our jaws stop clenching. We humans can be as unaffected as "The Rug" lying peacefully in the center of the room or on the big green couch, a calm presence. We can approach life's ups and downs with ease and a big lovely sigh of contentment, knowing everything is just as it's supposed to be.

BARKING BUDDHA POSES FOR EASE
Move into these poses with a sense of ease in your body. Start by relaxing your face. Dogs are keen observers

and often notice tension in our bodies and facial expressions. If you feel at ease, your dog will pick up on that and begin to relax.

Head to Knee/Muzzle to Paw

This pose is a forward bend. Forward bending poses calm the nervous system and tone the middle of the body. Forward bends also cultivate patience, an important quality in developing ease. Head to Knee/Muzzle to Paw also has the human benefit of lengthening the hamstrings and the doggy benefit of a leg muscle massage and stretch, which can be beneficial for circulation and muscle tension relief.

Come to a seated position, extending your left leg out in front of you. Bend your right knee and release it to the floor, out to the side, bringing the bottom of your right foot to your inner left thigh. Ideally your dog should be lying in front of your bent leg, but if your dog is standing, the pose will still work.

Engage your extended leg by flexing your left foot, toes pointed upward. Extend your spine from your pelvis, reaching forward with your heart. This

Head to Knee/Muzzle to Paw

Head to Knee/Muzzle to Paw, modification for standing dog

seated forward bend should grow from the sit bones, lengthening your spine and right hamstring. If you have a tight low back or hips, preventing you from sitting up straight before bending forward, sit on the edge of a folded blanket.

As you lengthen forward to stretch your hamstring, take your dogi's leg—it doesn't matter which leg you begin with—starting from the joint and gently stretch out his leg. You can also do a gentle squeezing action on his leg from the top of the leg to the paw.

Take a little time on the paw; it's helpful to get our dogs used to their paws being touched—it makes future nail trims a lot easier!

Take time to breathe with your doga partner and focus on his needs in the pose. Would he prefer to have his leg gently massaged or gently stretched? With a large dog you can use two hands; with a small dog use one hand. Do two of your dogi's legs as you're forward bending over your left leg, and then move to your other side. By the way, if your dog is standing during this pose, simply choose the massage option, no worries—we're practicing ease, right?

Puppy Pigeon

From Head to Knee/Muzzle to Paw, bend your extended leg so that it is bent behind you. Your legs should be in two little Vs, with your knees pointed in the same direction.

Puppy Pigeon

With your dogi lying in front of you, extend your spine from your pelvis until your chest is lightly resting on or near your dogi. This should be an easy hip stretch for you, so don't go further than your body allows. Take one hand and gently place it on your dogi's head, and place your other hand on his low back in Barking Buddha Mudra (or in Heart-to-Hound Mudra).

Begin to focus on your inhales and your exhales. Notice your dogi's breathing, how her breath mingles with your breath. Visualize your breath moving from your heart, down your arms, and out the palms of your hands, giving your dog healing energy and love. Your hands may begin to feel warm as you focus your energy and breath on your dogi.

Continue to focus your intention and your breath on giving healing and love to your dogi. Let your breath come easily. If you feel any tightness or stress in your chest, think of something about your dog that makes you smile, and let yourself smile as you take a deep inhale and exhale through an open mouth, releasing any tension.

Repeat the pose with your knees pointed in the other direction to give your hips a gentle stretch on both sides.

Dogi-Yogi Easy Pose

For this pose simply sit in a crossed-legged position on the floor with your dog by you or on your lap. If you have tight hips or a tight low back that prevents you from sitting up straight comfortably, sit on the edge of a folded blanket. You can also lean up against the wall. That's it . . . you're in the pose.

Dogi-Yogi Easy Pose, large dog variation

MEDITATION ON EASE

As you sit with your dog in Dogi-Yogi Easy Pose, let your face relax and take a nice deep breath, and then exhale through an open mouth. If that felt good, do it again. This will help release tension in your lungs and body, allowing tension to also be released in your mind. Give your dogi a big smile to set your intention of ease.

Begin to breathe in an easy manner with your mouth gently closed and your face and shoulders relaxed. Bring your mouth into a tiny Buddha smile, as smiling brings ease into almost any situation. Inhale your belly away from your spine; exhale your belly toward your spine. Notice how easily the breath finds its way in and out.

As you sit and easily breathe with your dogi, watch and acknowledge each thought that tries to take your attention from this moment of ease. Give the distracting thoughts a small, relaxed Buddha smile and let them float away from you without clinging or holding on to them.

Be in this way for as long as you like, and then give your Barking Buddha a treat and thank him for his assistance in your practice today. In the future, whenever you're feeling overwhelmed or stressed out, remember Lucy's serene, easy presence and how you too can adopt the same ease as "The Rug."

ENCOURAGEMENT

No one appreciates the very special genius of your conversation as the dog does.
—CHRISTOPHER MORLEY

DO YOU EVER HAVE THOSE DAYS when you feel like a sad, wandering stray dog? Or like one of those big-eyed dog paintings from the 1970s, the cartoonish ones with big heads and enormous eyes often painted on velvet with a forlorn look of "Why me?" I think we all have those big-eyed dog days brimming with second-guessing and self-pity.

They don't come around very often for me any-more (guess I'm a lucky dog), but when they do, I try to hole up at home and spend time with my canine counselors, Honey and Gus. That's the thing about dogs: They witness the worst and the best that humans have to offer and, amazingly, they stick around and offer support without even knowing it. Or maybe they do know it, in their own dog way.

Although I don't mind sharing these times with friends, I don't always say the right thing, and neither do they. But dogs speak volumes without voicing their opinions or, worse, giving unsolicited advice. They don't try to fix things. They're just there for us. Their devoted presence can be enough to encourage us to lighten the mood and make us feel like everything's going to be okay, because usually it will be.

Who wouldn't feel encouraged by Honey's presence?

The sympathetic looks, the soft and warm fur, the nonjudgmental listening, and the unconditional love are certainly all part of canine therapy. But there's also that sense from dogs of "Hey! Someone's gotta feed us and take us on a walk. That's your job! We can't open the closet where you keep our food! There's a leash law! We need you to take us out or we could end up like those strays!"

My dogs are my conscience. How can I wallow in self-pity when I look in those big brown eyes or see that encouraging tail wag? Sometimes it's not that easy to shake off a foul mood, but it should be. Honey and Gus remind me to take the drama down a notch. Look at what life has to offer, they say: green grass, a nice walk, kind words, and a sincere cuddle. These simple joys my dogs and I share always encourage me to take a deep breath and tackle whatever comes my way. And canine counseling is affordable—no deductible, except an extra treat or two!

BARKING BUDDHA POSES FOR ENCOURAGEMENT

It's fun to do these poses in a sequence, so do all of them on one side before moving to the other side.

Pit-to-Paw Standing Twist, small dog variation

Pit-to-Paw Standing Twist

Begin standing with your feet hip distance apart and your dogi in front of you, facing away. Slightly tuck your tailbone as you come into Half Up-Tail, a half forward bend with your spine parallel to the ground. Lightly rest your hands on your dogi's shoulders.

Keeping your spine parallel to the ground, place your right hand on your dogi's left shoulder. As your hand is massaging the shoulder bend your left arm and place your left hand on your back side. Draw your shoulders down your back and open up your chest to the side of the room by coming into a slight twist, pushing your left elbow toward the ceiling. Inhale, and on the exhale, let your hand travel from your dogi's shoulders to her paw until you are in a slightly twisted forward bend, called Up-Tail.

Take a couple of breaths and enjoy the opening of your spine and back. Then come back into Half Up-Tail for Wheelbarrow.

Wheelbarrow

In your half forward bend, let your hands travel down both sides of your dog to her hips. Gently lift your dogi from right under her hips, high in the hip crease, not in the middle of the leg. As you lift your dogi's back legs off the ground, she should get a nice hip and spine stretch. Gus likes to rest his back paws on my thighs and push into my legs so he really gets a nice extension in his spine and back legs. Keep your shoulders drawn back and lift your leg bones up and back so

Wheelbarrow, small dog variation

that your kneecaps are slightly lifted—this gives you a stretch as well.

If your dog is too large for you to lift, she would greatly appreciate a hip massage as you breathe in your half forward bend. For the hip massage, use a gentle circular squeezing motion with your hands either on top of her hips or on her inner legs, or both.

After you release your dogi, move into Lucky Dog Lunge.

Lucky Dog Lunge

From a standing position, move your right leg back into a low lunge. Your right knee can be on the ground, if that feels easier or if your dog is smaller. Keep your bent left knee aligned directly over your left ankle. Tuck your tailbone and lift your belly and chest up. Relax your shoulders. Sweep your arms up toward the sky, palms facing toward each other.

As your spine moves up and your shoulders and arms move down, reach your fingertips forward to your dog. Rest your hands on either side of her jaws. Give her a loving jaw massage by making gentle circles with your fingertips,

Lucky Dog Lunge is an excellent pose for the barkers and the chewers, since their jaw muscles get a lot of use. If your dog is really jowly, like my Honey, you may need to use your fingers or even your hand for the jaw work.

When you are finished, bring your left leg back so that you can stand up on your knees for Super Dog Twist.

Super Dog Twist

Stand up on your knees with your knees hip distance apart and your tailbone tucked. Lift your belly up and

Lucky Dog Lunge, with arm motions

Super Dog Twist, large dog variation

slightly in to engage your core, and keep your shoulders relaxing down your back.

Reach under your dogi's front legs, right up in the creases where the legs connect to her body. Lift her front legs, extending them straight out. Slowly and slightly, turn your torso to the left, just a little, and then to the right, just a little. Your dogi's torso should also be slightly twisting along with you.

If your dogi is too large to lift, gently place your hands on her shoulders. Softly push your right hand forward and gently pull your left hand back, and then move your hands in the opposite directions.

Breathe in Double Dog Down Dog or Puppy Child's Pose (both described in the Gratitude sequence) for a couple of breaths before moving through the poses on your other side.

71

DOGI: SADIE ROSE

Age: 3
Breed: Australian shepherd
Yogi: Denise
Sadie is obsessed with tennis balls, sleeps on Denise's bed with her head on the pillow, and lovingly washes her cat Hobbes's ears.

MEDITATION FOR ENCOURAGEMENT

Sometimes when we're feeling bad it's helpful to make someone else feel good, balancing out sadness or self-pity with something positive. Sit with your dogi and begin massaging her jaw muscle. You can feel where the jaw connects, and with some practice you'll begin to notice the tension in the muscle. Use gentle yet firm circular finger motions.

Begin to mindfully move your fingers/hands (depending on your dogi's size) down to her neck. You can do anything with a meditative quality, so focus your mind, breath, and intention on your dogi. Get outside of yourself and whatever is going on to discourage you and for now focus on your dog.

Continue to bring your mind and breath back to your intention of giving your dogi complete healing attention as you move your massage down to her shoulders. Continue to use gentle, firm, circular motions with your hands. Move to the sides of her body and eventually to her hips. Take your time. Notice where she is holding tension. What does she prefer: the neck massage or the hip massage? This is an opportunity to really connect to your dogi and do something nice for her.

After your meditation-massage, smile at your dogi; dogs are keen observers and like to see us smile. Now encourage a dog smile from your dogi by presenting her with a post-doga dog biscuit.

LIBERATION

I think we are drawn to dogs because they are the uninhibited creatures we might be if we weren't certain we knew better.

—George Bird Evans

IN YOGA, to liberate yourself is to completely free your mind from all unnecessary thought, thus reaching a state of nirvana, or bliss. Imagine how great it would feel to achieve that, to be free and clear of worry or obsession. Honey and Gus will occasionally become obsessed with the possibility of food or a walk. But, for the most part, they're seemingly free from worry or troublesome thoughts. They are pretty Zen.

I've tried to stand in their paws and imagine what it would be like to always wear a collar as they do, to be on a leash much of the time, and to live in that kind of bondage. It would be awful! But they don't seem to mind. It's part of their dogdom. In fact, whenever I take off Honey's collar, she gets a little freaked out; she noses the collar and looks at me like she doesn't understand the implications of being free from the leather encircling her thick, wrinkly neck.

The same goes for their leashes. Both Gus and Honey love me putting on their leashes because it means they get to go somewhere. But sometimes if I'm in an open space and I take off the leashes, they run, run, run! Later, when I call them back after this liberating romp, they come right to me and sit pa-tiently while I reinstate bondage, clipping the leashes back onto their collars.

Contemplating their collared and leashed existence, I began to compare the collar and leash to our human beliefs and thoughts. Like a collar, our beliefs are always there, comfortable, or at least familiar, encircling us, part of our identity. Likewise with the leash, our thoughts. We relish some of our thought patterns so much that we cling to them like a dog gnawing on or playing tug-of-war with his leash.

But if you can experience a moment when you're free from some of these patterns, when you can run around untethered from your obsessions, beliefs, and worries, it can bring an amazing sense of lightness, calm, and freedom. This sense of freedom rarely lasts. (That's why yogis and other spiritual seekers take years, even lifetimes, to achieve an enlightened existence.) We all usually go right back to the leash and collar that keep us bound to our familiar patterns, our established identity.

Maybe the trick is to stay aware of our patterns, our bondage, while we seek a liberating enlightenment, so that they don't pull us back from those freer moments—like Honey and Gus romping across an open meadow. Doga, yoga, and meditation offer a glimpse of a liberated mind and the feeling of peace that follows. Let's let our dogs help us loosen our collars and remove our leashes with the following poses.

BARKING BUDDHA POSES FOR LIBERATION

I associate the next three poses with freedom because they're physically and energetically expansive, bringing a sense of liberation as the body opens up physically and energetically expands outward. Our dogs respond to our energy as we expand—they are right there with us as we move through these powerful poses. It's fun to do all the poses on one side before moving to the other side.

Woofing Warrior 2, large dog variation

Woofing Warrior 2

To begin Woofing Warrior 2, come into a lunge but open your hips so that your chest and pelvis are facing the side of the room and your front (right) toes are facing the front of the room. Your back (left) foot is flat on the ground and your toes are angled slightly forward. Your tailbone is tucked and your heart and belly are lifted.

If your dog is large, he's inside your front bent knee or under your front thigh. Either way, he's there to remind you to keep that front knee moving out to the baby-toe side of your foot and not to splay inward toward him. You'll work on getting that front thigh parallel to the floor (it may not be today), lightly resting on your dogi if he's under your thigh—*lightly* . . . you're holding your own thigh up, your dog is not doing it for you. Spread you arms out like wings, palms facing down and shoulders moving down your back.

If your dog is small, he's sitting on your front thigh or you're holding him in your arms. Your back

Woofing Warrior 2, small dog variation

hand supports your dogi on your thigh or holds him to your heart, and your front arm extends over your front leg, palm down.

From either version, straighten your front knee to move into Xtra Angle Triangle.

Xtra Angle Triangle

This pose is easy to move into from Woofing Warrior 2 because your legs basically remain in the same stance, except that you straighten your right knee. If you're holding your dogi, set him down on the inside of your right leg.

Gently tuck your tailbone and lift your belly muscles to engage your core, and spread your arms like bird wings. Reach your right fingertips beyond your right foot to stretch both side waists long as you open your heart and hips.

As your heart reaches open toward the ceiling, let

Xtra Angle Triangle, modification without lifting paw

Xtra Angle Triangle, large dog variation

your top (left) hand reach up and your bottom (right) hand rest on your dog or lift his paw. You can also reach down and lift your dogi's paw so that his pose mirrors yours.

Expand out in all directions, but keep your gaze and energy directed to your doga partner. Take a couple of expansive, liberating breaths before flying into Dog Over the Moon.

Dog Over the Moon

This pose makes you feel like you're flying, and what better way to feel free than by flying? This pose is like Xtra Angle Triangle, except that you lift your back leg off the floor.

Keep your back foot flexed and continue opening your hips and chest by stacking them and drawing your

shoulders down. This pose definitely requires some balance, so feel free to stand with your back against a wall the first time you try it. You can also come down to one knee (**Puppy Over the Moon**). I recommend either of these options if you're a beginning yogi.

Your dogi can partner with you in this freeing pose in a couple ways. If you are comfortable with your balance, you can softly rest your hand on your dog, avoiding his spine or belly. Only do this if you are very sure of your balance in this pose. You can also use your doga partner as a point of focus. Steady your gaze on him as you hold the pose. (We gaze on something while balancing because it helps us keep steady.)

Balancing poses can be exhilarating, so after a few breaths with your dogi in the pose, reach both hands down to the floor. Quiet your mind in Double Dog

Dog Over the Moon, large dog variation

Puppy Over the Moon

Down Dog or Puppy Child's Pose (both described in the Gratitude sequence), and then you'll both be ready to move into Dogi-Yogi Easy Pose for meditation.

Dogi-Yogi Easy Pose

Simply sit in a crossed-legged position on the floor with your dog by you or on your lap. If you have tight hips or a tight low back that prevent you from sitting up straight comfortably, sit on the edge of a folded blanket. You can also lean up against the wall. That's it . . . you're in the pose.

Dogi–Yogi Easy Pose, small dog variation

MEDITATION FOR LIBERATION

If you like, take off your dogi's collar for this meditation to symbolically represent liberation. It can be freeing to do something that makes us feel a little uncomfortable. So after you've removed your dogi's collar, loosen your own collar and put on your favorite sing-along music. Anything you like—opera, hip-hop, new wave, sappy love songs—anything that brings up emotion. Emotion lets us free our minds.

Almost anything can be done in a meditative manner, so I want you to sing to your dog. That's right—sing to your dog. Really, I've done this—it's freeing and makes my dogis and me feel good. When you allow your mind freedom to express emotion in a healthy manner, you can more easily free yourself from that emotion instead of swallowing it or obsessing about it.

After your concert, sit with your dogi and rest in the vibration of the music as you watch your inhales and your exhales with a mind that is a little closer to liberation.

DIVINITY

Dogs are our link to paradise. They don't know evil or jealousy or discontent. To sit with a dog on a hillside on a glorious afternoon is to be back in Eden, where doing nothing was not boring—it was peace.

—MILAN KUNDERA

WE ALL KNOW THAT dog spelled backward is God, and most of us have heard the saying "dog is my copilot." It's a cute saying, but what gives? Are people trying to be irreverent or funny? Is there a deeper meaning that goes beyond the bumper sticker? The definition of *divine* according to Webster's dictionary is "of, relating to, or proceeding directly from God." *Divinity* is defined as "the quality or state of being divine" (interestingly, another definition is "fudge made of whipped eggs, sugar, and nuts"). My vote, then, is yes, there is a deeper meaning.

That definition of divinity reminds me of a woman I met in a coffee shop recently. She was telling me about her dog Butterscotch. I'll call her Coffee Shop Lady because I unfortunately don't remember her name, though, of course, I almost always remember a dog's name. Coffee Shop Lady and I were talking about the spirituality books she had been reading when (naturally) the conversation turned to dogs. She said that her Butterscotch was such a pure, loving spirit that whenever something challenging came up, instead of asking, "What would Jesus do?" Coffee Shop Lady would ask herself, "What would Butterscotch do?" I've never met Butterscotch, but I can imagine that the

wisdom and strength in her bright eyes surpasses that of many humans. Next time I'm challenged, maybe I'll also ask myself, WWBD? Couldn't hurt, right?

In yoga we talk about connecting to the divine in all living things. That includes dogs, cats, hamsters, birds, the peonies in our gardens, even grumpy people and screaming babies. But we do this by first connecting to the divine within ourselves. So here's a bone to chew on: What if we are everything divine, and everything divine is us? We are all divine and are having a divine experience in whatever ways we choose to live our lives. The divine experience we seek, consciously or not, is that connection to something pure and loving within ourselves.

Honey and Gus give me a glimpse of this by opening my heart, enabling me to connect to some small divinity in myself and then to experience it all around me. When we make a choice to wake up to the divinity in all things, we begin to understand the universal connection of everything. If we and all of our surroundings have the possibility of being divine, then, yes, dog is our copilot. Butterscotch, Honey, and Gus are all part of the community made of our divine dogs.

BARKING BUDDHA POSES FOR DIVINITY

Doga is a heart-opening practice. When we live life from the heart instead of the head, we are more able to acknowledge the divinity in all things because we don't get caught up in ego and fear. As you move from pose to pose, let your dogi assist you in focusing your intention on acknowledging the divine in yourself and your dogi. Just acknowledging the heart-opening qualities of the relationship you share with your dog can help you focus on your intention and broaden your understanding of what divinity means to you.

Heart-to-Hound Push-Up

This pose strengthens your chest and shoulders. Start on your hands and knees with your hands shoulder distance apart and your knees hip distance apart. If possible, your dogi should be between your hands, lying down if she's large.

Tuck your tailbone and lift your belly up and in. Draw your shoulders down your back, away from your ears toward your waist, which will help stabilize your shoulder joints. Try to keep your elbows close in to your ribs as you exhale your body down, bringing your heart in the direction of your dogi. Keeping your elbows close in is a little more challenging than letting them splay out, but it reduces the risk of injury and brings a nice alignment to the posture. It also makes for some nice, sculpted shoulder muscles you'll enjoy showing off later.

Do as many push-ups as you like, inhaling up and exhaling down, each time reaching your heart in the direction of your dog, metaphorically allowing her to help you feel a heart connection. You can also try to get down low enough to plant a little kiss on the top of your dogi's head. If you don't have the strength to lower down that far yet, make it a goal to work toward in your future Heart-to-Hound Push-Up practice.

Heart-to-Hound Push-Up

Double Dog Down Dog

After you've completed your Heart-to-Hound Push-Ups, curl your toes under and lift your hips up and back, moving into Double Dog Down Dog. In this pose, try to touch the crown of your head to your dogi. If it doesn't reach, that's okay. Let your intention be to open your mind to divine connection through the love you share with your dogi.

Lower your heels to the floor, straightening and opening up the back of your legs. Let your sit bones tilt up as you extend your arms, opening up your elbow creases and broadening your upper back. Relax your neck and breathe freely.

When you're ready, begin to walk your feet toward your hands for Dog Is My Copilot.

Dog Is My Copilot

Stand with your dogi in front of you. Stand tall with your core engaged by tucking your tailbone and lifting your belly up and in. Bring your weight to your left leg.

As you slightly bend your left knee, begin to hinge forward at your hips, reaching your arms toward the floor and extending your right leg out behind you. Keep the toes of your back leg pointing down so that your hips are square to the floor.

Reach down and place one hand on the floor, and if you feel very stable balancing on one leg, place your other hand lightly on your dogi. Gaze at your dogi to help you balance.

Seeing double during Double Dog Down Dog

Crash during Dog Is My Copilot!

Breathe here as you continue your intention of divine canine connection. When you've done the pose on both sides, come down to the floor for Puppy Pigeon.

Puppy Pigeon

Sit for a moment in Dogi-Yogi Easy Pose, legs crossed on the floor with your dog by you or on your lap. If you have tight hips or you have a tight low back, sit on the edge of a folded blanket.

Keep your right knee bent as you bend your left leg behind you. Your legs should be in two little Vs. Keep your spine lifting out of your pelvis as you place one hand on your dog's chest or between her shoulders and your other hand on your heart in Heart-to-Hound

Puppy Pigeon

Mudra. Heart-to-Hound Mudra acknowledges the love you and your dog share.

Try to feel an energetic connection between your heart and your dogi's heart, a balanced circular energy moving between you and your dog. Now that you've opened up the heart and mind connection, you and your dogi are ready to meditate.

MEDITATION ON DIVINITY

This meditation can be done in Puppy Pigeon or in any comfortable seated position with your dog in front of you. Place one hand gently on your dog's head or between his shoulders and one hand on his low back in Barking Buddha Mudra.

On the inhale, visualize light entering the crown of your head; when exhaling, picture the breath moving down into your heart, through your arms, and out the palms of your hands. Your hands may begin to feel warm as you bring your healing intentions to your dog with your breath and visualization.

After giving your dog this healing, divine energy, sit quietly and experience any healing energy your dog gives back to you. When this beautiful exchange is complete, thank your dogi and give him a heavenly post-doga treat.

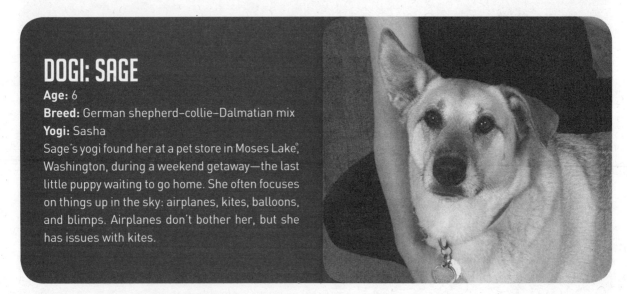

DOGI: SAGE

Age: 6
Breed: German shepherd–collie–Dalmatian mix
Yogi: Sasha
Sage's yogi found her at a pet store in Moses Lake, Washington, during a weekend getaway—the last little puppy waiting to go home. She often focuses on things up in the sky: airplanes, kites, balloons, and blimps. Airplanes don't bother her, but she has issues with kites.

PLAY

The dog was created specially for children. He is the god of frolic.
—HENRY WARD BEECHER

I LIKE TO START and end my classes by running around with the dogs. The goal is to get everyone, dog and human alike, to join me in a playful uninhibited romp around the room. Mostly, though, it's just me and the dogs; the human students just stand and watch. That's fine, I guess. But it makes me wonder: When did we decide to be uncomfortable with our playful selves? When did we decide that only children, dogs, and eccentrics get to embrace the silliness, the possibility, and the play of life? When did we all decide life was so serious?

I don't know the answers to these questions. But I do know that if we take a moment to embrace our inner dog and imagine that we've already learned everything we're going to learn, life will be more fun and will feel easier. Imagine for a moment that we're not here to learn but are here to play. Let's take the pressure off and give ourselves permission to be like our dogs—playful and in the moment. You can voice many responsible reasons why this can't be. But try it anyway!

If you tell yourself you already know everything, you can relax and spend time discovering that knowledge within, letting it unfold so that life becomes a

Playtime means get up and run!

DOGI: GRCH 'PR' LARUM'S TEMPTIN TROUBLE U-WP, A.K.A. "TROUBLE"

Age: 3
Breed: American pit bull terrier
Yogi: Emily

Trouble is a UKC Grand Champion and is currently the ninth top-winning show pit bull in the country. In her spare time, she enjoys giving hugs and pulling the "cream filling" out of stuffed toys.

time of awakening and self-discovery and not such hard work. You can go play.

BARKING BUDDHA POSES FOR PLAY AND MEDITATION

Put worries, work, deadlines, bills to pay, chores to do, and, yes, your ego aside for a while. Don't let daily concerns prevent you from discovering your inner dog. Give yourself permission to play and romp about.

Let's begin our play practice by running around with our dogs, laughing and getting a little breathless. Be very present. Believe that nothing is more important right now than playing with your dog. Find a dog toy and throw it for your dogi or play a game of chase. Bark, howl, roll in something stinky! Well, maybe don't roll in something stinky, but do call forth that inner dog. And when you find her or him, reward yourself with the treat of fun and silliness. This will lighten your energy and make your dogi happy, because she's there to support you on your journey to self-discovery.

There . . . that's your pose *and* your meditation.

LETTING GO

My little dog—a heartbeat at my feet.

—EDITH WHARTON

DOCILE FROM BIRTH, Gus will duck his head and roll onto his back for almost anyone. He has no apparent fear, yet he doesn't try to hold onto any role of dominance. I adopted Gus from a small-dog rescue shelter in Blaine, Washington. I found him online. Well, I found his pregnant mother online and applied to adopt one of her puppies . . . Baby Gus. I became the expectant mother . . . of a puppy. I've had Gus since he was born. I even visited him before he was ready to come home and met the birth mother so we could all get to know each other. And on the day I picked him up to bring him to his new home, I immediately started to socialize him. Gus's first stop in Seattle was our local dog-friendly coffee shop.

Over the next few weeks and months, I introduced him to a lot of different situations: man in a hat, person on bicycle, small child. At the dog park little Gus would want me to pick him up, and although I was tempted to scoop him up protectively, I stayed strong and made him play with the other dogs.

I'm proud that he's now so well-adjusted. I can take him anywhere without worrying about his behavior. He seems mostly to associate strangers and new places with dog treats. Even still, people will sometimes comment that he's shy or scared when they first meet him, because he displays behavior that's subservient, like lowering his head. They just don't understand. I patiently explain that Gus is neither shy nor scared. His personality is naturally docile and he has never been given any reason to show aggression, so he moves into a compliant role. He doesn't need to be aggressive. Gus is simply able to let go and roll over.

What if we could experience life in the same way? Instead of giving in to fears and trying to control our worlds, what if we could just let go and let life happen? When we can let go of expectations, the need to control, or the fear of the unknown, we're able to see things with more clarity and to make choices in life that aren't forced or based on fear. Without clinging to our fears and "what ifs," we open up to new things entering our lives. We can play, experience, and receive. Like Gus, all we need to do is roll over and let go.

BARKING BUDDHA POSE FOR LETTING GO

Try doing these poses without interruption. Turn off your cell phone, dim the lights, limit the risk of distraction so you can really roll over and relax. Be present in the peaceful atmosphere you've created, focused only on relaxing with your dogi for a few undisturbed minutes.

Roll Over and Relax

Basically that's all you need to do here. Roll over and relax. Lie on your back, with your dog close to you. Close your eyes and let go. The lying down is the easy part, the letting go, not so much. So let's move right into the meditation as we lie here to help us with the letting go.

MEDITATION FOR LETTING GO

The meditation for letting go is very simple. Lying in Roll Over and Relax with your dogi, begin to use a simple mantra with your breath. We can use this particular mantra to help us let go of any thoughts that are preventing us from letting go. Inhale on the word "let," exhale on the word "go." Your dogi can partner with you in this process as you breathe with him.

Roll Over and Relax, large dog variation

Roll Over and Relax, small dog variation

Notice how easily he is able to let go and be in your loving presence as you surrender to the healing and love he offers unconditionally. As thoughts, worries, and fears try to sneak in and prevent you from being fully present in the meditation, continue to use the mantra to bring you back to your intention.

Try to stay in the pose for at least 5 minutes. Notice how peaceful you feel after being able to let go of anything getting in the way of being fully present for you and your dogi. Smile, laugh, play, and enjoy this new awareness, then give your dogi his after-doga treat.

HONEY AND GUS GOULASH RECIPE

I FEED THIS CONCOCTION to Honey and Gus once or twice a week to vary their meals. I like to feed them twice a day. I'll feed this to them in the morning and give them dry kibble at night. Feed your dog something new for his morning meal or mixed into his regular kibble. Either way, it's easier on your dog's digestion when you're introducing new things into his diet.

2 cups cooked brown rice

2 tablespoons nutritional yeast flakes

1 cup frozen peas (add them to the warm rice to heat them up just right)

1 cup minced or shredded carrots

1 tablespoon fish or flax oil

1 cup vegetable or chicken broth

2 teaspoons canine multivitamin powder (or as directed on package)

Optional: any combination of raw egg, dry kibble, other minced or shredded veggies, and/or a little shredded cheese (not recommended for doggies on a diet)

Mix everything together in a big bowl. Be sure the rice is cool before you add the other ingredients (besides the peas) and especially before feeding the goulash to your dog. Portion size varies depending on dog size. If you have a small dog, you may have enough for a few meals.

Opposite: Gus and Honey love their goulash!

ACKNOWLEDGMENTS

I'D LIKE TO OFFER my sincere gratitude to my family and friends. Thanks to Brad, Brenda Barnette and the Seattle Humane Society, Bev Sparks, Kate Rogers at Skipstone, the Downtown Dog Lounge, Seattle Dogis and Yogis, and the dog lovers who have emailed me from all over the world extending their support and encouragement. Most of all, I give my deepest, heartfelt thanks and treats to dogs everywhere.

DOG PHOTOGRAPHY

Bev Sparks specializes in the fine art of photographing dogs. In addition to private commissions, her work is used by publishers, ad agencies, greeting card companies, and non-profits and was featured on "The Oprah Winfrey Show." Her other books include *Dog Park Wisdom: Real World Advice on Choosing, Caring For, and Understanding Your Canine Companion* and *Unleashed: Climbing Canines, Hiking Hounds, Fishing Fidos, and Other Daring Dogs,* both by Lisa Wogan, and *Busy Doggies,* by John Schindel. You can contact Bev via her website, www.dogphotography.com.

Opposite: Puppy Over the Moon

RECOMMENDED RESOURCES

NOTE: I'm always discovering new and cool dog-friendly businesses and yoga venues, including yoga studios that offer doga classes utilizing my instruction methods. Please check my blog, www.dogyoga.blog spot.com, for updates and current doga information.

DOG ORGANIZATIONS

The Delta Society (www.deltasociety.org)
Fur Baby Rescue (www.furbabyrescue.com), an organization specializing in small-dog rescue. This is where I got Gus.
The Humane Society of the United States (www.humanesociety.org)
Petfinder (www.petfinder.com)

BOOKS AND MEDIA

Dog Park Wisdom, by Lisa Wogan (Skipstone, 2008). Provides great real-world advice.
Doga: Yoga for Dogs, by Jennifer Brilliant and William Berloni (Chronicle Books, 2003). This is a cute book with many photos of dogs doing their own version of yoga.
For the Love of a Dog: Understanding Emotion in You and Your Best Friend, by Patricia McConnell, Ph.D. (Ballantine Books, 2006). This woman gets dogs.
The Healing Touch for Dogs: The Proven Massage Program for Dogs, by Dr. Michael W. Fox (Newmarket Press, 2004).

"It's Me or the Dog," an Animal Planet program featuring Victoria Stilwell. I like her dog training style except, contrary to her advice, I do let my dogs sleep with me—sorry, Victoria! Her show is entertaining and helpful, and she also has books and DVDs available on her website (www.victoriastilwell.com).
The Other End of the Leash, by Patricia McConnell, Ph.D. (Ballantine Books, 2003). For more of her books and DVDs, visit www.patriciamcconnell.com.

DOGA

Dogs Dig It, Portland, Oregon (www.dogsdigit.net). Portland's favorite doggy daycare now teaches doga.
Royce Gallery, San Francisco, California (www.roycegallery.com). The Royce hosts innovative dance classes—and will soon offer doga.

DOG-FRIENDLY ESTABLISHMENTS

Downtown Dog Lounge, Seattle, Washington (www.downtowndoglounge.com)
The Inn at Cape Kiwanda, Pacific City, Oregon (www.innatcapekiwanda.com). Check my website for upcoming doga retreats at this canine-friendly inn on the Oregon Coast.
The Kimpton Group Hotels, with locations across North America (www.kimptonhotels.com)

Opposite: Profiles of Woofing Warriors!

BARKING BUDDHA DOGA™

TRADITIONAL YOGA IS all about creating "Union"—that is, attaining a connection to the divinity in all things.

Dogs make great yoga partners because they are pack animals to begin with, and pack mentality is based upon cooperation, connection, and understanding. In a doga practice, we partner with our dogs, using them as a catalyst to an easier heart connection. Through this intimate dog–person relationship, we can experience a broader connection to the pack, to all things . . . Union.

Although the path is similar to that of a traditional yoga practice, it's important to acknowledge that with our dogis, we will walk a little differently. This is doga, after all, and it's more playful and organic. Our four-legged dogis sometimes run or pull on the leash while on the path to discovery! But by first opening up our hearts and connecting to them, we can find that connection to our divine selves as we might through traditional yoga. Discovering divinity is simply finding the very best part of yourself that is creative, loving, and feels a connection, a union, to all around you.

Barking Buddha Doga uses stretches, massage, and simple meditations to connect and unify on both an emotional and a physical level—and it benefits both dogi and yogi. Dogs love the massage and stretching they receive in doga class, which is great for their circulation and tension. They also learn to be touched and to socialize with other dogs and people. And, of course, they love getting undivided attention from their humans.

For the human yogis, the benefits of stretching and relaxation are similar. The added bonus is that dogs help us experience life from the heart instead of through the head. They show us how to open ourselves up, foster that heart connection, and bring it into other aspects of our lives.

Barking Buddha Doga is a fun and energetic way to experience a deeper human–canine union and to relax the world, one dog at a time.

WWW.BARKINGBUDDHADOGA.COM
WWW.DOGYOGA.BLOGSPOT.COM

ABOUT THE AUTHOR

WHEN BRENDA BRYAN BEGAN practicing yoga in the late 1990s, she was very inflexible. Although she found yoga to be one of the most difficult things she had ever tried, she continued to attend classes and work toward gaining the flexibility to reach down and touch her toes.

She continued her yoga practice for several years, experiencing a wide variety of teachers and styles, before enrolling in a teacher training program herself at 8 Limbs Yoga in Seattle, Washington. While honing her teaching skills, Brenda, a licensed massage therapist, also studied small animal massage. Ultimately, she found a way to combine her love for yoga and for dogs by adapting a series of yoga poses to do with your dog at your side. Barking Buddha Doga classes are partner classes that combine classic Hatha yoga poses with gentle stretching and massage for your canine companion. Benefiting yogi and dogi, the class is structured to bring awareness to the connection you have with your dog and a deepening of that very special relationship.

Brenda currently teaches yoga classes for both people and dogs throughout the Seattle area; her own dogs Honey and Gus assist her in teaching the dog classes. She also leads teacher training seminars in the methods she developed for Barking Buddha Doga and travels widely giving demos and interviews. She lives in Seattle with Honey, Gus, and her husband, Brad.

Brenda and her dogis, Honey and Gus

Time to put the doga mat away?